Sports Illustrated KIDS

Baseball

Then to WOW!

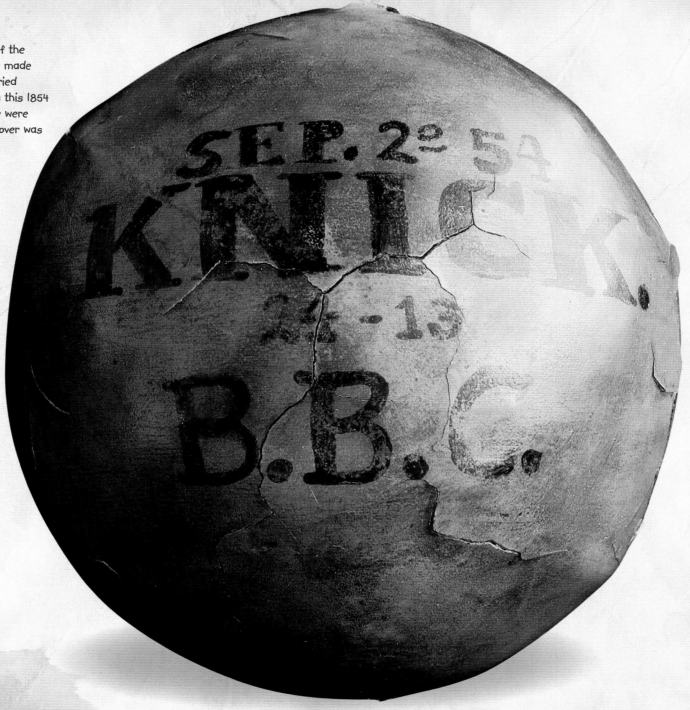

In the earliest days of the game, baseballs were made by hand, and they varied widely in size. And, as this 1854 specimen shows, they were often used until the cover was about to fall off.

THEN

Today's major league balls weigh between 5 and 5¼ ounces and are between 9 and 9¼ inches in circumference. The average game ball has a life span of seven pitches before it is taken out of play.

NOW

Managing Editor, Sports Illustrated Kids **Mark Bechtel**

Creative Director **Beth Bugler**

Writers **Mark Bechtel, Elizabeth McGarr McCue**

Photo Editors **Annmarie Avila, Linda Bonenfant**

Copy Editor **Pamela Ann Roberts**

Reporter **Ben Baskin**

Premedia **Geoffrey Michaud, Dan Larkin, Gerry Burke, Brian Mai, Sandra Vallejos**

Illustrations by **Andrew Roberts**

Published by Liberty Street, an imprint of Time Inc. Books
225 Liberty Street
New York, New York 10281

LIBERTY STREET and SPORTS ILLUSTRATED KIDS are trademarks of Time Inc.

ISBN 10: 1-61893-142-3
ISBN 13: 978-1-61893-142-9
Library of Congress Control Number: 2015955043

First edition, 2016

1 TLF 16

1 3 5 7 9 8 6 4 2

Time Inc. Books products may be purchased for business or promotional use. For information on bulk purchases, please contact Ilene Schreider in the Special Sales Department at (212) 522-3985.

To order Time Inc. Books Collector's Editions, please call (800) 327-6388,
Monday through Friday, 7 a.m.-9 p.m., Central Time.

We welcome your comments and suggestions about Time Inc. Books.
Please write to us at:
Time Inc. Books
Attention: Book Editors
P.O. Box 62310
Tampa, Florida 33662-2310

timeincbooks.com

Contents

The Basics

Baseball's origins have long been disputed, but one thing is certain: Since its birth the sport has brought people of all ages together to play and to cheer — whether at a cow pasture or a packed ballpark of 50,000. The written rules, established in their earliest form in 1845, have evolved over the years, and so have the equipment and the uniforms. (Boy, there have been some silly-looking outfits.)

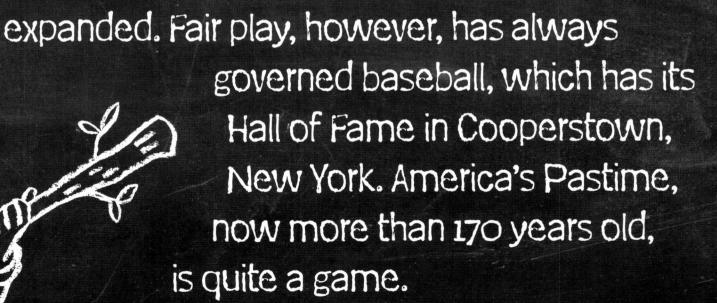

Even the reach of the game, which was first played exclusively on the East Coast, has expanded. Fair play, however, has always governed baseball, which has its Hall of Fame in Cooperstown, New York. America's Pastime, now more than 170 years old, is quite a game.

THE RULES

How the game has been played

I f you traveled in a time machine back to 1845 and landed on a baseball field, chances are you'd still recognize the game being played. Major rule changes are far more common in, say, football and basketball than they are in baseball. But there have been several tweaks, usually to make the game safer or more competitive. Some new rules have benefited pitchers, while others have given batters the advantage.

1845

Alexander Cartwright of the Knickerbocker Base Ball Club of New York City writes the Knickerbocker rules, which have evolved into the current rules of Major League Baseball. Included are setting the bases approximately 90 feet apart and giving each team three outs per inning.

1884

Overhand pitching is allowed. Because underhand pitching places little stress on the arm, some underhand pitchers in the early days completed as many as 70 games in a single season.

1887

Batters can no longer request the height at which they want the pitch to be thrown.

1889

The four-ball, three-strike rule is established. (That's a big difference from the rule in 1879, when a walk was nine balls!)

1891

Teams are now allowed to substitute as many players during the game as they want. But — unlike in basketball and football — once a player leaves the game, he cannot return.

1893

Instead of throwing the ball from a line drawn 50 feet away, the pitcher now has to keep his back foot on a slab of rubber 60' 6" from home plate.

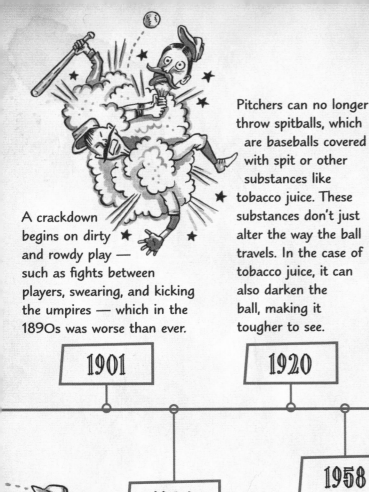

A crackdown begins on dirty and rowdy play — such as fights between players, swearing, and kicking the umpires — which in the 1890s was worse than ever.

1901

Pitchers can no longer throw spitballs, which are baseballs covered with spit or other substances like tobacco juice. These substances don't just alter the way the ball travels. In the case of tobacco juice, it can also darken the ball, making it tougher to see.

1920

American League owners increase the schedule from 154 games to 162. The NL follows suit a year later.

1961

The AL adopts the designated hitter rule, allowing a batter to hit for a pitcher. The NL votes against it.

1973

Baseball becomes the last of the four "major" North American sports to employ instant replay.

2008

1903

Foul balls are now counted as strikes in the American League. (The NL had adopted the rule in 1901.)

1958

After 100 years in which ballparks could vary as much as 150 feet in dimensions, minimum fence distances are established for new ballpark construction. They include a distance of 325 feet to the foul poles and 400 feet to centerfield.

1969

After a year of unprecedented pitching dominance, the highest part of the strike zone is moved from the top of the batter's shoulders to his armpits. Additionally, the pitching mound is lowered from 15 inches to 10.

1975

Players gain a huge victory over owners when they win the right to free agency. This makes it possible for players to sign with a new team after their contracts have expired. Before then, owners imposed a reserve clause, which bound the player to a single team as long as the team wanted to keep him.

2014

Replay is expanded, as managers are given one challenge per game.

The TEAMS

Tracking the franchises

Formed in 1876, the National League is the older of the two major leagues. Originally composed of eight teams, the NL — or the senior circuit — fluctuated in size until 1900, when it shrunk from 12 back to eight. It stayed that way for more than half a century. Until after the '57 season, all eight of those teams were in the eastern or central part of the country. But that changed when the Dodgers and Giants moved from New York to California. The first major expansion came in '62, when two teams were added — including the Mets, who brought NL baseball back to the Big Apple. Three subsequent expansions brought the league's roster to 16 teams until the Astros moved to the American League in 2013 to put the NL at its current size: 15 franchises.

Seattle

Brew Crew

The Milwaukee Brewers not only began their existence in a different city, they began it in a different league. The Seattle Pilots were founded in 1969, but they only spent one season in the Emerald City before moving to Wisconsin. After 28 seasons in the American League, the Brewers joined the NL in 1998.

see you later!

Colorado Rockies
1993–present

San Francisco Giants
1958–present

Los Angeles Dodgers
1958–present

San Diego Padres
1969–present

Arizona Diamondbacks
1998–present

National League

Traveling Braves

One of two remaining charter members of the National League (along with the Cubs), the Braves have played in three cities: Boston (where they shared top billing with the Red Sox), Milwaukee (where they preceded the Brewers), and Atlanta.

Montreal

Boston

1970: Pilots move to Milwaukee and become the Brewers

Milwaukee Brewers
1970–present

1953: Braves move to Milwaukee

2005: Expos move to Washington and become the Nationals

New York Mets
1962–present

958: Giants move from New York to San Francisco

Chicago Cubs
1876–present

• **Philadelphia Phillies**
1883–present

Dodgers move from Brooklyn to Los Angeles

Pittsburgh Pirates
1887–present

1966: Braves move to Atlanta

Cincinnati Reds
1882–present

958: Dodgers move from Brooklyn to Los Angeles

St. Louis Cardinals
1882–present

Washington Nationals
2005–present

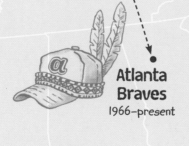

Go West!

For more than 80 years, no major league team played west of St. Louis. That changed after the 1957 season, when the New York Giants and Brooklyn Dodgers decided to tap into the California market. The Giants went to San Francisco, and the Dodgers made Los Angeles their new home.

Atlanta Braves
1966–present

Take Three

After losing two American League teams, Washington, D.C., got a senior circuit franchise in 2005. The Montreal Expos, which had become Major League Baseball's first Canadian team in 1969, made the move south and became the Nationals.

Miami Marlins
1993–present

⇒ Today ⇐
Divisions

The NL split into two divisions in 1969 and added a third in '94. This is how the teams are currently aligned:

East
Atlanta Braves
Miami Marlins
New York Mets
Philadelphia Phillies
Washington Nationals

Central
Chicago Cubs
Cincinnati Reds
Milwaukee Brewers
Pittsburgh Pirates
St. Louis Cardinals

West
Arizona Diamondbacks
Colorado Rockies
L.A. Dodgers
San Diego Padres
San Francisco Giants

The TEAMS

The American League became a "major" league in 1901, giving the National League its first real competition. Because it did not have a maximum salary, the AL was able to attract many star players from the NL. In 1903, the two league champions met in the first World Series, which became a yearly occurrence in '05. Like the NL, the AL began with eight teams. Following each of the first two seasons, an AL team relocated. The Milwaukee Brewers became the St. Louis Browns in 1902, and then in '03 the Baltimore Orioles became the New York Highlanders (and, later, the Yankees). After that, the league was stable until 1954, when the Browns moved to Baltimore — and called themselves the Orioles! (Got all that?) The league expanded to 10 teams in 1961 and 12 teams in '69. By 1998 it was up to 14 teams, and it got its 15th and final franchise, the Houston Astros, in 2013 when Major League Baseball decided to make the two leagues the same size.

Seattle Mariners
1977–present

1968: Athletics move to Oakland

Oakland Athletics
1968–present

Los Angeles Angels of Anaheim
1961–present

Roaming A's

The Athletics have called three cities home over the last century-plus. They spent 54 seasons in Philadelphia, then moved to Kansas City in 1955. After flirting with several cities, including Louisville and Dallas, the A's hit the road again in '68, headed for Oakland.

American League

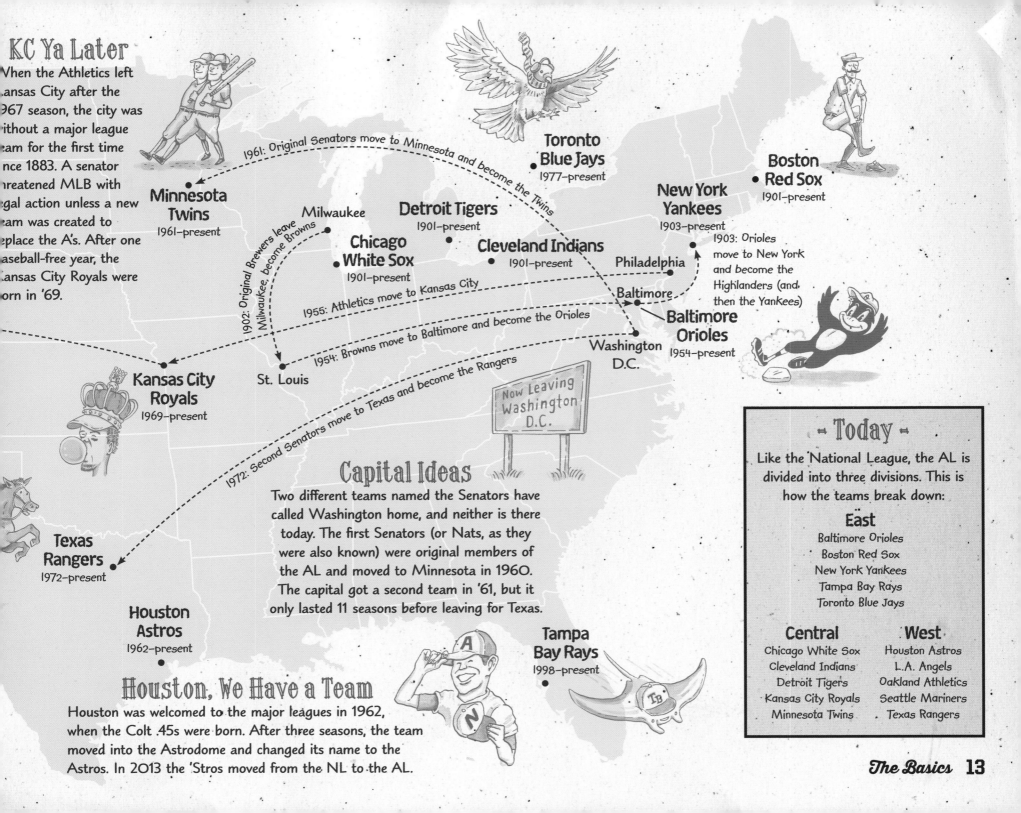

KC Ya Later

When the Athletics left Kansas City after the 1967 season, the city was without a major league team for the first time since 1883. A senator threatened MLB with legal action unless a new team was created to replace the A's. After one baseball-free year, the Kansas City Royals were born in '69.

1961: Original Senators move to Minnesota and become the Twins

Toronto Blue Jays
1977–present

Boston Red Sox
1901–present

Minnesota Twins
1961–present

Milwaukee

Detroit Tigers
1901–present

New York Yankees
1903–present

1903: Orioles move to New York and become the Highlanders (and then the Yankees)

1902: Original Brewers leave Milwaukee, become Browns

Chicago White Sox
1901–present

Cleveland Indians
1901–present

Philadelphia

Baltimore

1955: Athletics move to Kansas City

Baltimore Orioles
1954–present

1954: Browns move to Baltimore and become the Orioles

St. Louis

Washington D.C.

Kansas City Royals
1969–present

1972: Second Senators move to Texas and become the Rangers

Now Leaving Washington D.C.

Capital Ideas

Two different teams named the Senators have called Washington home, and neither is there today. The first Senators (or Nats, as they were also known) were original members of the AL and moved to Minnesota in 1960. The capital got a second team in '61, but it only lasted 11 seasons before leaving for Texas.

Texas Rangers
1972–present

Houston Astros
1962–present

Houston, We Have a Team

Houston was welcomed to the major leagues in 1962, when the Colt .45s were born. After three seasons, the team moved into the Astrodome and changed its name to the Astros. In 2013 the 'Stros moved from the NL to the AL.

Tampa Bay Rays
1998–present

≈ Today ≈

Like the National League, the AL is divided into three divisions. This is how the teams break down:

East
Baltimore Orioles
Boston Red Sox
New York Yankees
Tampa Bay Rays
Toronto Blue Jays

Central
Chicago White Sox
Cleveland Indians
Detroit Tigers
Kansas City Royals
Minnesota Twins

West
Houston Astros
L.A. Angels
Oakland Athletics
Seattle Mariners
Texas Rangers

No one was getting dressed in a hurry thanks to these lace-up jerseys ...

... and ties!

Many early jerseys were collarless.

UNIFORMS

Dressing for success on the diamond has meant many different things through the years

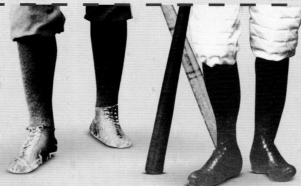

Who needs a uniform when you can just play in your dress pants?

1860s

1880s→90s

1900s

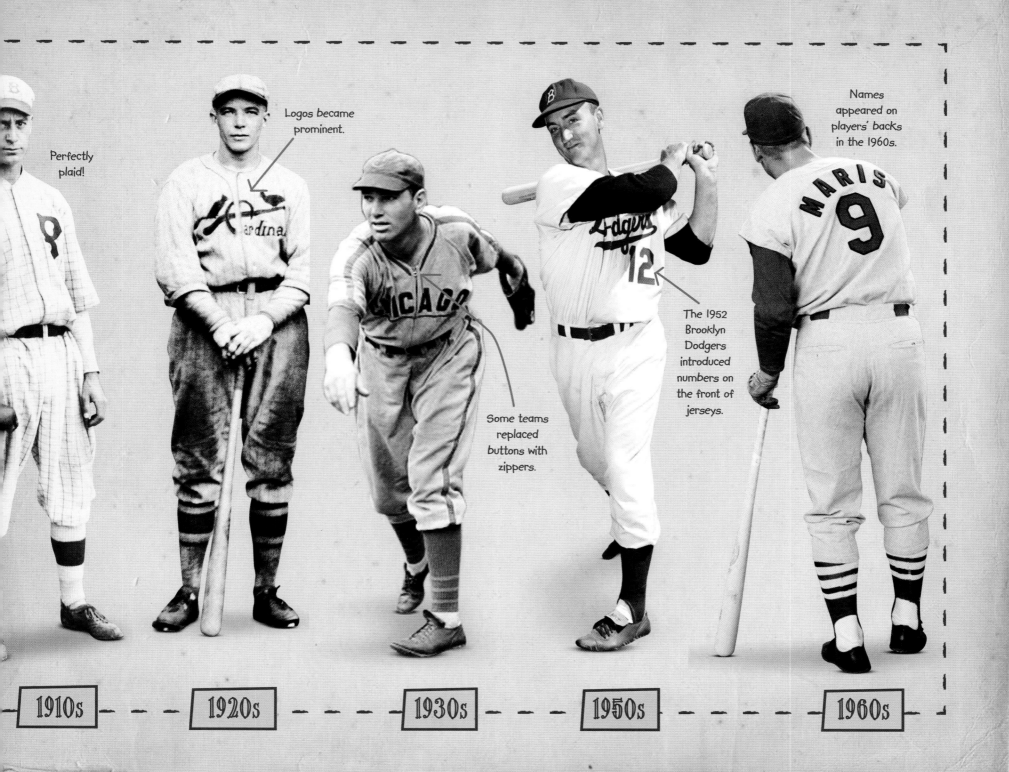

Perfectly plaid!

Logos became prominent.

Some teams replaced buttons with zippers.

The 1952 Brooklyn Dodgers introduced numbers on the front of jerseys.

Names appeared on players' backs in the 1960s.

1910s — — — 1920s — — — 1930s — — — 1950s — — — 1960s

The 1970s featured some of baseball's wildest ensembles. The Pittsburgh Pirates wore gold pants and pillbox hats.

The 1970s were also a great decade for daring 'dos and mustaches.

The Chicago White Sox experimented with shorts in 1976.

The Houston Astros set the standard for colorful jerseys.

PIRATES 8

CHICAGO

INDIANS

Astros 21

1970s

Many teams dropped their traditional gray road outfits for baby blue.

Classic-looking uniforms returned.

The baggy look took over.

Teams seem to be trying to outdo one another with uniforms created in a wild throwback style.

1980s 1990s 2000s 2010s

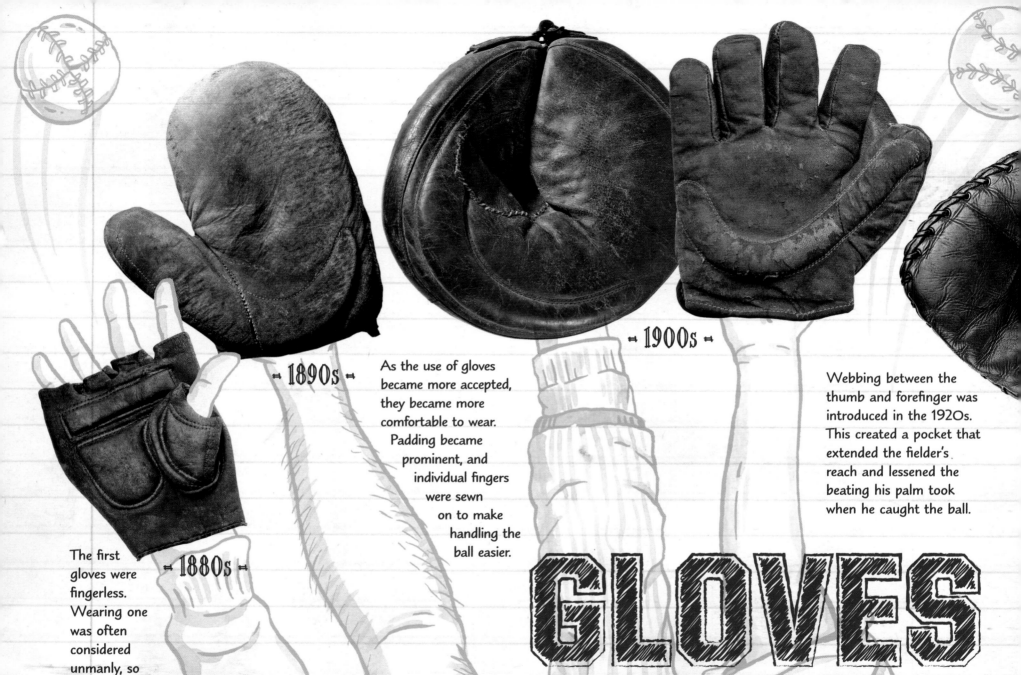

= 1890s =

= 1900s =

The first gloves were fingerless. Wearing one was often considered unmanly, so players wanted them small and difficult to notice.

= 1880s =

As the use of gloves became more accepted, they became more comfortable to wear. Padding became prominent, and individual fingers were sewn on to make handling the ball easier.

Webbing between the thumb and forefinger was introduced in the 1920s. This created a pocket that extended the fielder's reach and lessened the beating his palm took when he caught the ball.

GLOVES

Catch up on the history of the gear that players use to catch the ball

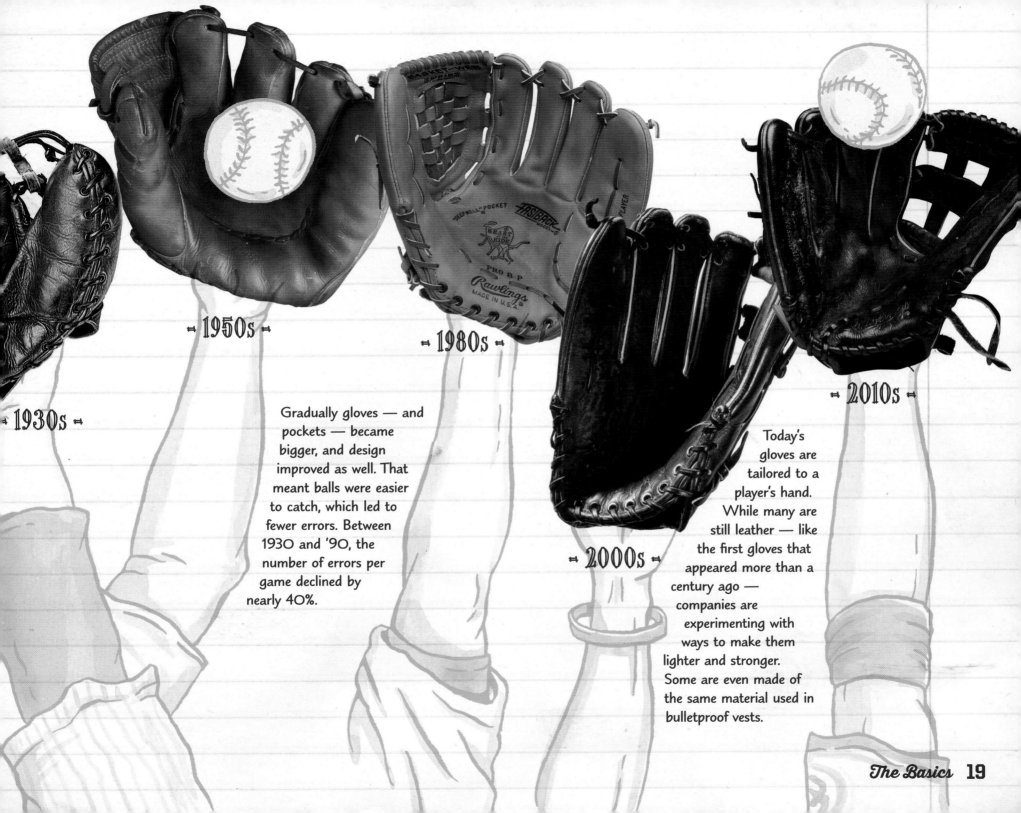

= 1930s =

= 1950s =

= 1980s =

Gradually gloves — and pockets — became bigger, and design improved as well. That meant balls were easier to catch, which led to fewer errors. Between 1930 and '90, the number of errors per game declined by nearly 40%.

= 2000s =

= 2010s =

Today's gloves are tailored to a player's hand. While many are still leather — like the first gloves that appeared more than a century ago — companies are experimenting with ways to make them lighter and stronger. Some are even made of the same material used in bulletproof vests.

CATCHER'S

Until the mid-1870s, catchers played bare-faced. The earliest masks were called rat traps.

Eventually masks came to be accepted. Improvements included making them stronger and, thanks to padding, more comfortable.

❖ 1870s ❖

❖ 1880s ❖

❖ 1920s ❖

❖ 1940s ❖

MASKS

How backstops protect themselves from foul balls — and bats

After L.A. Dodgers catcher Steve Yeager was hit in the neck by a broken bat in 1976, the team's trainer developed a throat protector that attached to the mask.

The first hockey-style masks were used in the 1990s. Modern-day masks protect a catcher's entire head while allowing him to see better.

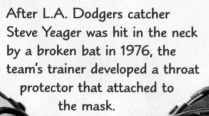

⇥ 1970s ⇤   ⇥ 1980s ⇤   ⇥ 1990s ⇤   ⇥ 2010s ⇤

STADIUMS

The splendid parks that major league teams call home

Fenway Park
Boston Red Sox
(1912–present)

Dodger Stadium
Los Angeles Dodgers
(1962–present)

Veterans Stadium
Philadelphia Phillies
(1971–2003)

Metrodome
Minnesota Twins
(1982–2009)

Classic Designs

In the early days of the game, baseball stadiums were built wherever land could be found. Often that meant fields were wedged into odd-shaped areas. At Fenway Park, for instance, the rightfield foul pole is just 302 feet from home plate, but the fence in deep centerfield is 420 feet away. Meanwhile, the leftfield wall is 310 feet away — and 37 feet tall!

Baseball-only

As the major leagues expanded and franchises moved in the 1950s and '60s, teams had to find new homes. After spending their first four seasons in L.A. in a cavernous football stadium, the Dodgers moved into a state-of-the-art park in 1962. Dodger Stadium is now the third-oldest park in the majors, but its great sight lines still make it one of the most popular.

Multipurpose

Building a stadium is not cheap, so in the 1960s and '70s many cities constructed facilities that could house both baseball and football teams. As a result, the parks tended to be big and round, in order to accommodate both field configurations. Since they all looked as if they were made from the same circular mold, they were dubbed cookie-cutter stadiums.

Dome Sweet Dome

Baseball's first indoor stadium, the Astrodome, opened in 1965. The plan originally was to grow grass under the roof, but when that failed, artificial turf — called AstroTurf — was installed. When the Twins moved into their dome in 1982, they realized that the ball seemed to carry better indoors. Soon the park was known as the Homerdome.

Old Meets New

Starting in the 1990s, old-time, retro parks began appearing in Baltimore, Cleveland, and other cities. This new wave of parks blended traditional elements with modern touches. Nowhere is that more evident than at Seattle's Safeco Park, which opened in 1999.

⇇NOW⇉

Staying Dry

Seattle is one of the rainiest cities in the country, so before moving to Safeco, the Mariners played in a dome. Their new stadium allows them to play outside, but if the weather is threatening, it has a roof that can cover the field in 10 to 20 minutes.

What's the Score?

Safeco features a manual scoreboard in leftfield for out-of-town games. It is operated by hand, just as scoreboards were 100 years ago. But Safeco also features the largest high-definition replay screen in the majors, which measures a whopping 201 feet wide!

The Players

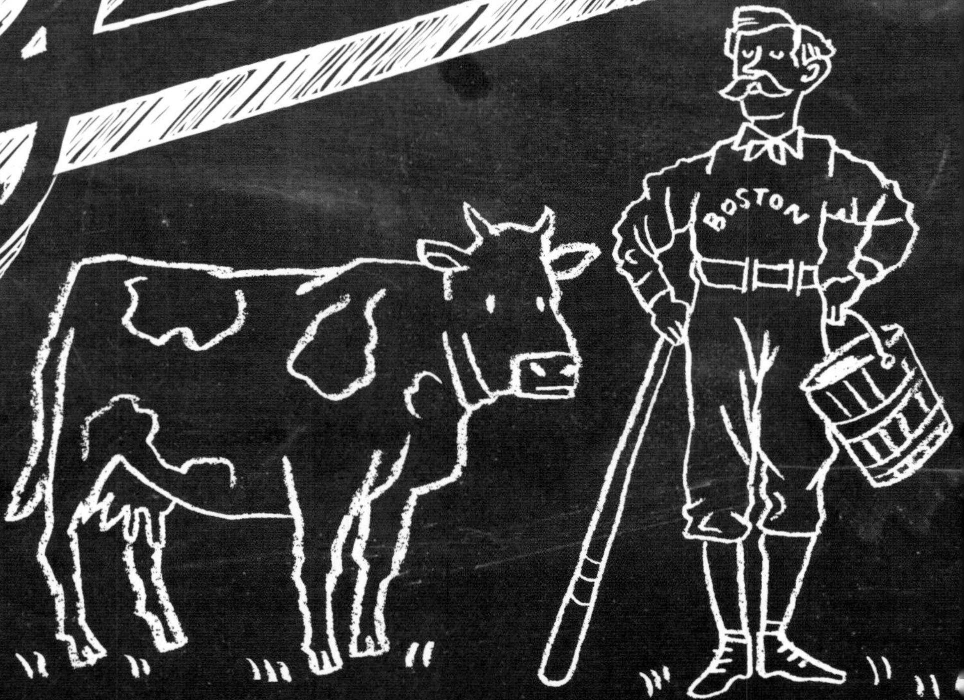

Who had the sweetest swing in baseball? What about the swiftest stride? From the hottest hitters of all time to speedsters who could round the bases at blistering paces, the game has always been made better by those who play it. There have been quotable characters, pitchers who had pizzazz, trailblazing pioneers, and once-in-a-generation talents who could simply do it all. Meet the biggest stars from baseball's past and present.

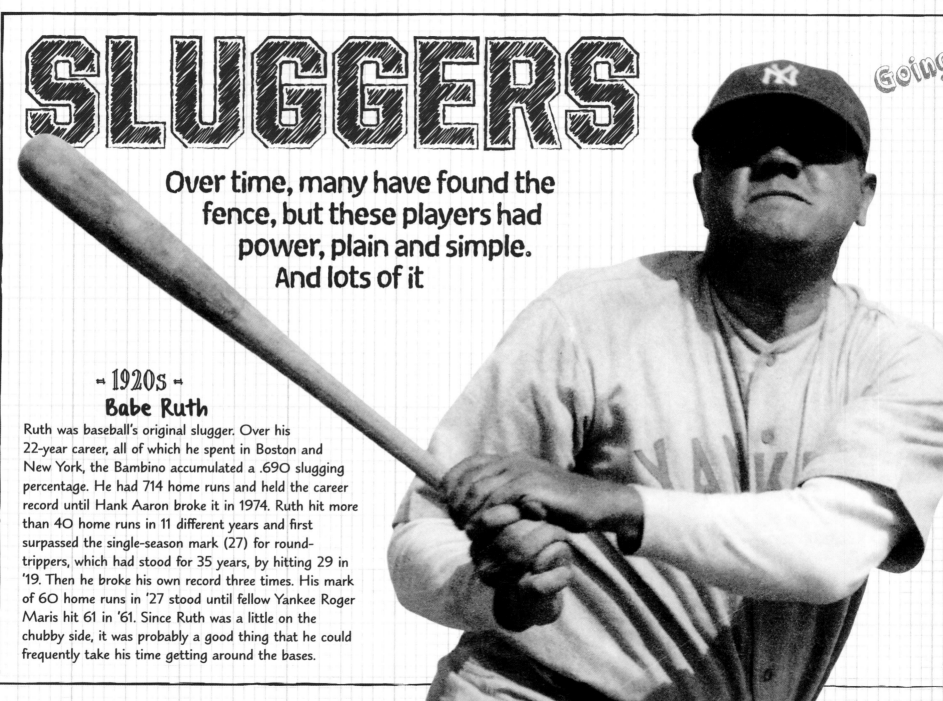

SLUGGERS

Over time, many have found the fence, but these players had power, plain and simple. And lots of it

⇒ 1920s ⇐
Babe Ruth

Ruth was baseball's original slugger. Over his 22-year career, all of which he spent in Boston and New York, the Bambino accumulated a .690 slugging percentage. He had 714 home runs and held the career record until Hank Aaron broke it in 1974. Ruth hit more than 40 home runs in 11 different years and first surpassed the single-season mark (27) for round-trippers, which had stood for 35 years, by hitting 29 in '19. Then he broke his own record three times. His mark of 60 home runs in '27 stood until fellow Yankee Roger Maris hit 61 in '61. Since Ruth was a little on the chubby side, it was probably a good thing that he could frequently take his time getting around the bases.

Going, GONE!

⇔ 1930s ⇔
Lou Gehrig

He wasn't called the Iron Horse for nothing. Not only did Gehrig play in 2,130 straight games for the New York Yankees from June 1925 through April 1939, but the first baseman also led the AL in slugging twice and in RBIs five times. He retired in '39 because he was suffering from amyotrophic lateral sclerosis (ALS), which affects a person's ability to move by attacking his or her nervous system. He died two years later from the illness, which is now often called Lou Gehrig's disease.

It's Outta Here!

⇔ 1940s ⇔
Jimmie Foxx

Foxx built his strength by working on his father's farm in Maryland, where he grew up excelling in baseball, as well as track, soccer, volleyball, and basketball. He played his first game in the majors when he was only 17 and had won the first of his three MVP awards by the time he was 24. He was nicknamed the Beast because he could hit the ball so far. Joked Hall of Famer Lefty Gomez, who pitched against Foxx, "When Neil Armstrong first set foot on the moon, he and all the space scientists were puzzled by an unidentifiable white object. I knew immediately what it was. That was a home run ball hit off me in 1937 by Jimmie Foxx."

Ted Williams

The Kid was known for his better-than-perfect eyesight. (His vision was 20/10, which is even sharper than 20/20.) That helped the lifetime Boston Red Sox leftfielder win six AL batting titles over his 19-year career. He trails only Babe Ruth in slugging percentage.

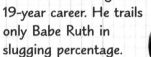

A Four-Bagger!

⊨ 1950s ⊨
Willie Mays

The Say Hey Kid was one of the most dynamic and talented players the game has ever seen. In centerfield, he was strong, speedy, and had a great arm. He could also knock the heck out of the ball, as evidenced by his 660 home runs (he's fourth on the all-time list) and .557 lifetime slugging percentage. He was an All-Star for 19 straight years beginning in 1954, when he returned from serving in the Army during the Korean War.

What a Tater!

⊨ 1960s ⊨
Hank Aaron

His nickname tells you all you need to know. Hammerin' Hank entered the Atlanta Braves' 1974 home opener with 714 home runs, tied with Babe Ruth for most all time. (Unfortunately, some people were angry that Aaron, an African-American player, might break Ruth's record.) L.A. Dodgers lefty

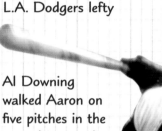

Al Downing walked Aaron on five pitches in the second inning that day. Facing Downing in the fourth inning, Aaron sent the ball into the leftfield bullpen, and fireworks filled the sky. He ended his career with 755 home runs.

⊨ 1980s ⊨
Mike Schmidt

When Schmidt retired, he had 1,883 strikeouts, third most in major league history. Uh-oh! Things didn't always go poorly for him, though. He also hit 548 four-baggers. Only the Babe himself won more home run titles than Schmidt, who led the NL eight times. His 48 homers in 1980 were the most ever by a third baseman at the time.

÷ 1990s ÷
Ken Griffey Jr.

His famous dad didn't hit with quite as much power when he made it big in the bigs back in the 1970s, but Junior? He knocked the ball out of the park more than any other American Leaguer during four seasons. And he hit 56 home runs two years in a row, in '97 and '98. He won seven Silver Slugger awards and also 10 straight Gold Glove awards for his work in centerfield.

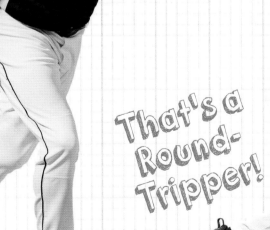

That's a Round-Tripper!

÷ 2000s ÷
Albert Pujols

It was clear when he became the NL Rookie of the Year in 2001 that Pujols was destined to become one of the game's great power hitters. After all, he had hit a grand slam in the first game he played in college. He led the NL in slugging percentage three times, in home runs twice, earned three MVP awards, and helped the Cardinals to two World Series titles.

÷ 2010s ÷
Miguel Cabrera

You could call him King Cabrera because he wears a crown. A Triple Crown, that is. In 2012, he became the first player in 45 years to win the batting Triple Crown, meaning he led the AL in batting average, home runs, and RBIs. The 10-time All-Star has won the AL batting title three times and reached 30 homers during nine of his 13 seasons in the majors.

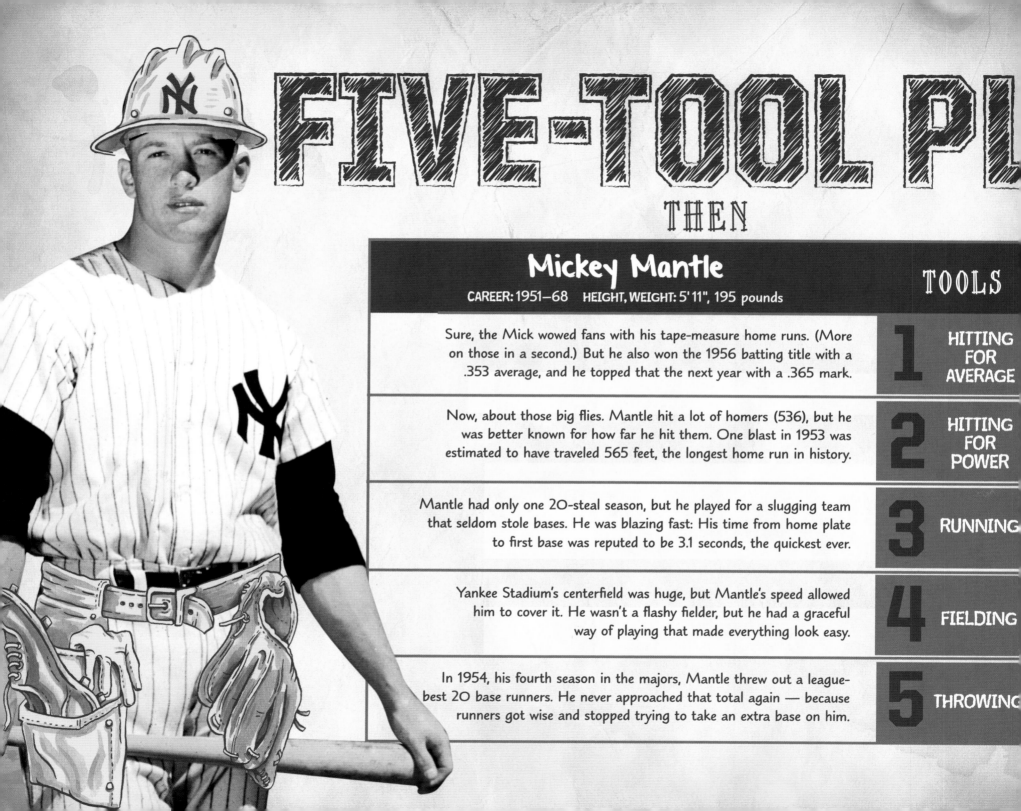

FIVE-TOOL PL

THEN

Mickey Mantle

CAREER: 1951—68   HEIGHT, WEIGHT: 5'11", 195 pounds

Sure, the Mick wowed fans with his tape-measure home runs. (More on those in a second.) But he also won the 1956 batting title with a .353 average, and he topped that the next year with a .365 mark.

1 HITTING FOR AVERAGE

Now, about those big flies. Mantle hit a lot of homers (536), but he was better known for how far he hit them. One blast in 1953 was estimated to have traveled 565 feet, the longest home run in history.

2 HITTING FOR POWER

Mantle had only one 20-steal season, but he played for a slugging team that seldom stole bases. He was blazing fast: His time from home plate to first base was reputed to be 3.1 seconds, the quickest ever.

3 RUNNING

Yankee Stadium's centerfield was huge, but Mantle's speed allowed him to cover it. He wasn't a flashy fielder, but he had a graceful way of playing that made everything look easy.

4 FIELDING

In 1954, his fourth season in the majors, Mantle threw out a league-best 20 base runners. He never approached that total again — because runners got wise and stopped trying to take an extra base on him.

5 THROWING

Some athletes can just do it all on the field and at the plate. Here's how two centerfielders match up

Mike Trout

CAREER : 2011—present   **HEIGHT, WEIGHT:** 6' 2", 230 pounds

The Millville Meteor (nicknamed after his New Jersey hometown) hit .326 in his rookie season. It was the highest batting average by a 20-year-old rookie since Ted Williams hit .327 — 73 years earlier.

Trout hit 77 homers over the 2014 and '15 seasons — and most seemed gone the moment they left his bat. Fifty-four of his taters traveled at least 400 feet, including one into the fountains in Kansas City in '14 that went 489 feet, the longest in the majors that season.

What was more impressive about Trout's season on the base paths as a rookie? That he stole a league-best 49 bases? Or that he was caught only five times? Either way, that's some pretty good running.

Trout hit 30 homers in 2012 — and took away several more, leaping and reaching over the fence to rob multiple hitters. That's typical of Trout's aggressive, highlight-heavy play in centerfield.

While he hasn't thrown out many base runners, Trout has done a decent job holding them. He has vowed to work on his arm strength — and he's shown that when he puts his mind to something, there's a good chance he'll do it.

HIT MEN

No player has hit better than .400 in a season since 1941. These guys came close, though

George Brett (1973-93)

He spent his 21-season career with the Kansas City Royals, reaching .390 during his AL MVP run in 1980, one of 13 seasons that he was named an All-Star and one of three years he won the AL batting title.

Tony Gwynn (1982-2001)

The amiable Mr. Padre was at .396 by the time the 1994 season ended and never hit below .309 following his rookie year. After winning eight NL batting titles, he coached baseball at San Diego State, where he had been an outfielder, as well as a point guard on the basketball team.

Roberto Clemente (1955-72)

An excellent outfielder with a rifle for an arm and speed on the base paths, Clemente hit a whopping .414 to help the Pittsburgh Pirates win the 1971 World Series. He is in the 3,000 hit club and paced the NL in batting four times.

Rod Carew (1967-85)

Carew, who had 3,053 hits, was a seven-time AL batting champion and an 18-time All-Star. He hit .350 or better five times, including his 1977 AL MVP year, when he ended the season sitting on .388.

Pete Rose (1963-86)

Rose didn't have the most powerful swing, but he won three NL batting titles and retired with more hits than anyone in the history of baseball (4,256). In 1989, he was banned from MLB for betting on the game.

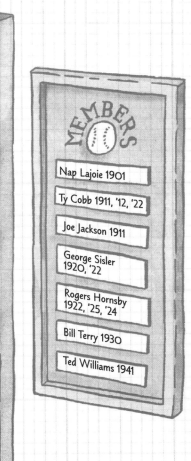

The .400 Club

MEMBERS

Nap Lajoie 1901

Ty Cobb 1911, '12, '22

Joe Jackson 1911

George Sisler 1920, '22

Rogers Hornsby 1922, '25, '24

Bill Terry 1930

Ted Williams 1941

Wade Boggs (1982-99)

The epitome of consistency, Boggs passed .360 in four different seasons and reached base in 80% of the games he played over his 18-year career. He retired with 3,010 hits.

Stan Musial (1941-44, '46-63)

Stan the Man led the NL in batting seven times and hit .357 or better in each of his three NL MVP seasons. He also paced the league in hits six times, doubles eight times, and triples five times. In other words, Musial could get on base!

Barry Bonds

Of course he's known for owning the all-time home run record. But Bonds also won eight Gold Gloves during a nine-season stretch in the 1990s — with the Pittsburgh Pirates and the San Francisco Giants — that included three NL MVP awards. (He was named MVP four straight years in the 2000s, too.)

LEFTFIELDER

Brooks Robinson

Well, when your nickname is the Human Vacuum Cleaner, that pretty much sums it all up. Few hits got past this lifelong Baltimore Oriole at the hot corner, and he's got the 16 straight Gold Gloves to prove it. Robinson was the 1964 AL MVP.

THIRD BASEMAN

Ozzie Smith

The man they called the Wizard of Oz obviously belongs on this list. He set major league records for assists and double plays turned at shortstop. He could also turn a pretty awesome backflip, which he did on the field nearly every Opening Day, All-Star Game, and postseason game.

SHORTSTOP

CENTERFIELD

GLOVE WIZARDS

Pop at the plate? Sure, these players had it. But they were also recognized for the nifty things they did in the field. Meet the nine stars on the all-time all-defensive team

Willie Mays

The Say Hey Kid made one of the most famous catches of all time, in the 1954 World Series against the Cleveland Indians. He caught a well-hit ball to centerfield over his shoulder, holding a runner at third in a 2–2 game. His New York Giants won the game and the Series.

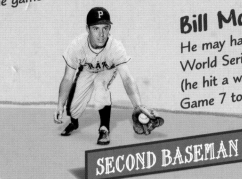

Roberto Clemente

Before he used his right arm to scare runners into slowing down on the base paths,

RIGHTFIELDER

Clemente threw the javelin for his high school track and field team. Tragically, the native of Puerto Rico died in a plane crash while traveling from his home country to Nicaragua with supplies to help victims of an earthquake.

Bill Mazeroski

He may have won the 1960 World Series with his bat (he hit a walk-off home run in Game 7 to help the Pittsburgh Pirates beat the New York Yankees), but Mazeroski is remembered as one of the best all-around fielders the game has ever seen. Even after he had spent only one year in the majors, SPORTS ILLUSTRATED referred to his "near-magical" abilities at second.

SECOND BASEMAN

Greg Maddux

He won four straight NL Cy Young Awards and more Gold Gloves (18) than any player ever. In 23 years on the mound, Maddux was a guy teammates could count on: He spent only 15 days on the disabled list.

PITCHER

FIRST BASEMAN

Keith Hernandez

Hernandez, mustache and all, was a reassuring presence at first base for the St. Louis Cardinals and the New York Mets in the 1970s and '80s, helping each team win a World Series. He earned NL MVP in '79 and picked up 11 Gold Glove awards. He began broadcasting games for the Mets on television in '99.

Johnny Bench

The 1968 NL Rookie of the Year just kept getting better. By the time he retired, after 17 years with the Cincinnati Reds, he had back-stopped the Big Red Machine to four NL pennants and two World Series wins and had picked up two NL MVP nods for himself. Base runners thought twice about trying to steal against Bench.

CATCHER

FLAMETHROWERS

⇔ 1910s ⇔
Gravity Drop Interval Recorder

The fastball is the simplest pitch in the game. The pitcher rears back and throws the ball as hard as he can. It's not about finesse. It's about raw power. And when a fan sees a hurler with a good fastball — someone who can throw gas, or bring heat — it's natural to want to know just how fast the ball is being thrown. The king of the heater in the early days of the game was Walter Johnson. The Big Train led the American League in strikeouts 12 times, and his career mark of 3,509 whiffs stood for 56 years. In 1917, he went into a laboratory where a fancy device called a gravity drop interval recorder measured his top speed of 91 miles per hour — though it is likely that a more accurate device would have produced a much higher speed.

⇔ 1940s ⇔
Motorcycle

Known as Rapid Robert, Bob Feller exploded onto the scene with the Cleveland Indians in 1936, when he was just 17 years old. Two years later, he won the first of four consecutive AL strikeout titles. In 1940, Feller "raced" his fastball against a motorcycle over a distance of 60' 6". (That's how far the pitcher's mound is from home plate.) He timed his release so that he threw the ball just as the bike was passing him at 86 miles per hour. Feller's pitch beat the ball to the plate handily. So handily, in fact, that its speed was calculated at 98.6 miles per hour!

91 MPH

Walter Johnson

98.6 MPH

Bob Feller

Which pitchers have thrown the hardest through the years? And more important, how have we been able to tell?

⇄ 1970s ⇄
Radar Gun

Before the 1970s, various mechanical devices were used to measure speed, but they were generally big and required pitchers to throw in special surroundings. That changed in 1973 when a college baseball coach got the idea to use the portable radar guns that the police used to catch speeding cars to measure the velocity of pitches. At the time, the hardest thrower in baseball was Nolan Ryan. The California Angels wanted to stage a promotion to see just how fast the Ryan Express was, so in '74 they brought in engineers to use radar to gauge him. Ryan's top pitch was 100.9 miles per hour, which was listed at the time in the *Guinness Book of World Records* as the fastest pitch. Ryan continued to dominate hitters for years, pitching until he was 46 and striking out 5,714 batters — 839 more than any other pitcher.

100.9 MPH

Nolan Ryan

⇄ Today ⇄
PITCH-f/x

For nearly a decade, major league stadiums have been equipped with PITCHf/x, a system that uses a pair of cameras to track the release point, spin, trajectory, location, and speed of every pitch. It does it in real time, to within one mile per hour and one inch. So now we know how much the best curveball breaks and how much a knuckleball flutters. And, of course, who throws the hardest: Aroldis Chapman. In 2010, the lefthanded reliever for the Cincinnati Reds uncorked a pitch that traveled an amazing 105.1 miles per hour. In '14, his fastball averaged 100.2 miles per hour for the entire season, when he struck out nearly two batters per inning.

105.1 MPH

Aroldis Chapman

PITCH MASTERS

These pitchers didn't throw the hardest, but with their specialized secret weapons, they were among the toughest to hit

NOW
Clayton Kershaw

THEN
Sandy Koufax

Curveball

NOW
Kenley Jansen

THEN
Mariano Rivera

Cutter

There's some debate over the best nickname for the curveball. The hook. The deuce. The yakker. Uncle Charlie. There's little argument about who threw it best: Koufax, who became the first pitcher to win five straight league ERA titles. That's one more than fellow Dodgers lefty Kershaw, who in 2014 won his third Cy Young Award and became the first pitcher to be named NL MVP in 46 years.

Rivera was one of the most predictable pitchers in history. For 19 seasons with the Yankees, he threw cut fastball after cut fastball. Hitters knew it was coming, and they still couldn't hit it. The hard pitch moved in on the wrists of lefthanded hitters and tailed away from righties. The late movement made it very difficult to hit solidly. Rivera retired in 2013 with a major-league-record 652 saves — the same season Jansen, relying heavily on his cutter, logged 28 saves for the Dodgers.

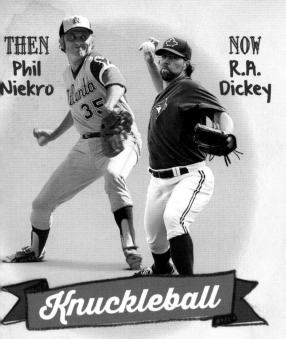

Knuckleball

The knuckleball floats through the air with almost no spin, so nobody is quite sure where it's going to go. In fact, it's as hard to catch as it is to hit. (One backstop said the best way to catch one was to "wait until it stops rolling and then pick it up.") Niekro predictably threw a lot of wild pitches and walked a lot of hitters, but he also is one of just 10 pitchers with 300 wins and 3,000 strikeouts. The pitch doesn't strain the arm much. Niekro lasted until he was 48. And Dickey, who adopted the pitch when it looked as if his career was ending, won his first Cy Young Award in 2012 — at age 37.

Slider

Carlton once said he was put on the planet to "teach the world how to throw a slider." But even with a lesson from the master, no one threw it like he did. The pitch looks like a fastball and then dives at the last second, leaving hitters swinging over the top of it. For a time Carlton held the career strikeout record, and he was the first player to win the Cy Young Award four times. Darvish has baffled hitters with a slider that's different from Carlton's. While it dives like Lefty's did, it also breaks sharply from right to left. It's no wonder that in Darvish's first three seasons in the majors, no one averaged more strikeouts per game.

Changeup

Most closers rely on the hard stuff, but Hoffman saved 601 games thanks to the slowest pitch of all. He'd set hitters up with a fastball and then throw what looked like another heater — except it was going about 12 mph slower. He tricked batters by using the same arm motion but lifting three fingers off the ball, slowing it down. These days, no one confuses hitters more than King Felix, a six-time All-Star.

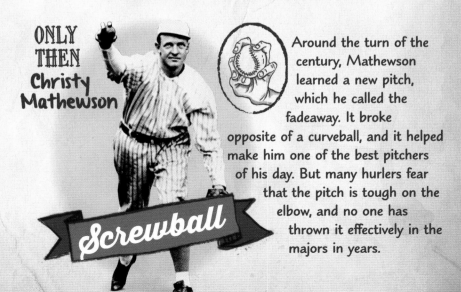

Screwball

Around the turn of the century, Mathewson learned a new pitch, which he called the fadeaway. It broke opposite of a curveball, and it helped make him one of the best pitchers of his day. But many hurlers fear that the pitch is tough on the elbow, and no one has thrown it effectively in the majors in years.

⌐ 1980s ⌐
Rickey Henderson

An All-America running back in high school, Henderson went on to become the Man of Steal, the greatest leadoff hitter of all time. He stole a major-league-record 1,406 bases and set the modern single-season mark with 130 in 1982 while with the Oakland A's.

⌐ 1970s ⌐
Lou Brock

Not only did Brock pace the NL in stolen bases eight times, but he also racked up 3,023 hits. He had 13 hits for the St. Louis Cardinals during the 1968 World Series, still tied for the major league record, and 12 the year before.

⌐ 1990s ⌐
Kenny Lofton

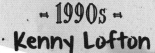

The onetime University of Arizona point guard took his neat footwork and quickness to the diamond, where few could rival his speed and effectiveness as a leadoff hitter. He topped the AL in stolen bases from 1992 through '96 and earned four Gold Glove awards in centerfield, helping the Indians win the '95 pennant.

There's fast, and then there are these guys. Quick! Take a look at the fastest players the game has ever seen — before they run off the page!

⌐ 2010s ⌐
Billy Hamilton

Pitchers are on high alert whenever the Cincinnati Reds' young centerfielder is on base. He's dangerous when he takes a lead off a base — in his first 165 games he stole second 55 times and third 14 times — and he'll likely get home from third on a sacrifice fly, even one to shallow leftfield. He hasn't stolen home … yet.

SPEEDSTERS

⊨ 1960s ⊨
Maury Wills

One of 13 kids, the switch-hitting Wills was a master of the bunt and had the speed to beat out more than a few throws to first after laying one down. He reached base on a bunt attempt with the bases empty a league-leading 18 times in 1965, three seasons after he stole 104 bases and became the NL MVP with the L.A. Dodgers. He led the league in steals from '60 through '65.

⊨ 1950s ⊨
Luis Aparicio

Aparicio made his mark in the majors on the field (retiring with more assists and double plays than any other shortstop) and on the base paths (he led the AL in steals during each of his first nine seasons). The 1956 AL Rookie of the Year with the Chicago White Sox became the first player from Venezuela to be elected to the Hall of Fame.

⊨ 1910s ⊨
Max Carey

The player called Scoops made quite an impression with the Pittsburgh Pirates at only 23 years old, stealing 61 bases and scoring 99 runs to lead the NL in both categories. He used his keen observations of pitchers' movements on the mound to lead the league in steals nine more times. Carey went on to manage the Brooklyn Dodgers in the 1930s and later two teams in the All-American Girls Professional Baseball League.

⊨ 1940s ⊨
George Case

This pitcher turned outfielder used his feet to make defensive plays and to become the top base runner of the decade, leading the AL in steals six times while with the Washington Senators and the Cleveland Indians before retiring at 31.

PIONEERS

Since its birth in America in the 19th century, baseball has evolved into a more inclusive sport. Meet the players who helped make MLB the diverse league it is today

African-American Players

Jackie Robinson became the first African-American to appear in the majors when he suited up at first base for the Brooklyn Dodgers on April 15, 1947. He endured taunts and boos from fans, hate mail, and discrimination everywhere he went, but he was named NL Rookie of the Year after leading the league in stolen bases. Two years later, he was named MVP. Fifty years after Robinson's debut, Major League Baseball retired his number, 42. (Thirteen players were allowed to keep the number until the end of their careers. New York Yankees pitcher Mariano Rivera was the last to wear it, in 2013.) The AL integrated shortly after the NL did. Less than three months after Robinson first played for the Dodgers, Negro leagues star Larry Doby took the field in his first game for the Cleveland Indians. Both Robinson and Doby are in the Hall of Fame.

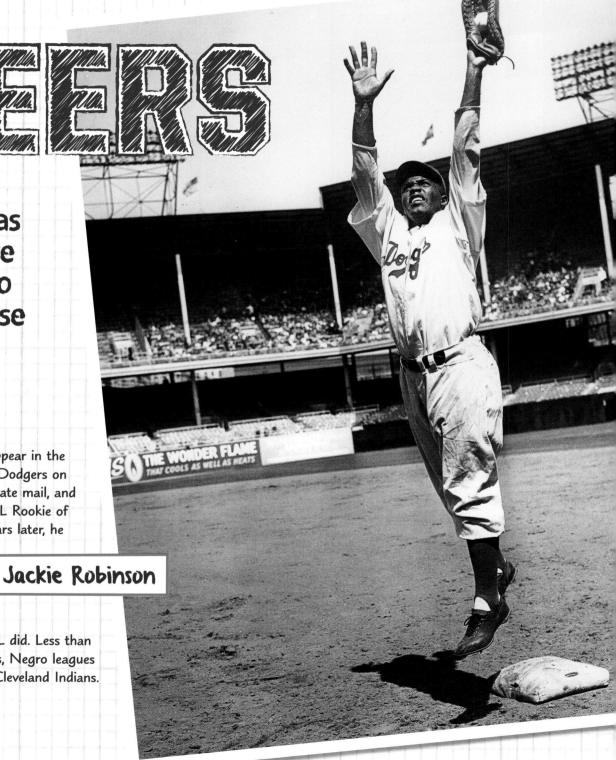

Jackie Robinson

Players from Latin America

Born in Havana, Cuba, Esteban (Steve) Bellán *(far right, second row)* became the first Latin-born player to reach a well-known professional league when he signed with the Troy Haymakers of the National Association in 1868. Latino players did not face all the same challenges as African-American players, but it was still a long time before anyone from Latin America really made it big in the majors. Dolf Luque was the first to do so, enjoying a 20-year career that began in 1914. He won 27 games for the Reds in '23 with an NL-best 1.93 ERA. Minnie Minoso became the first black Latino player to reach the majors, two years after Jackie Robinson did. There are fewer than a dozen Latino players in the Hall of Fame, but today nearly 25% of all major leaguers were born in a Latin American country. The one represented the most on 2015 Opening Day rosters was the Dominican Republic, with 83.

Esteban Bellán

Players from Japan

Masanori Murakami

In 1964, Masanori Murakami became the first athlete from Japan to reach the majors. Over two years as a reliever with the San Francisco Giants, he went 5–1 with nine saves. He returned to Japan after the '65 season and played another 17 years there. It wasn't until Hideo Nomo signed with the L.A. Dodgers in '95 that another Japanese player made the majors. Nomo was absolutely dominant, pitching one no-hitter for L.A. and one for the Boston Red Sox over his 12-year career. Nomo is one of several Japanese players to make an impact on American baseball over the last two decades, as is Ichiro Suzuki (the 2001 AL MVP and a 10-time All-Star and Gold Glove winner playing mostly in rightfield) and outfielder and designated hitter Hideki Matsui (the '09 World Series MVP with the New York Yankees). On Opening Day 2015, there were nine players from Japan on MLB rosters and also three from South Korea and one from Taiwan.

CHARACTERS

These one-of-a-kind spirits impacted the game with their mouths, their wit, and their appreciation of a good show

It ain't braggin' if you can back it up.

Age is a question of mind over matter. If you don't mind, it doesn't matter.

It ain't over till it's over.

Three Wise Men of Baseball

Dizzy Dean

The ace pitcher was a member of the dominant and colorful St. Louis Cardinals Gashouse Gang that won the 1934 World Series. He played with great enthusiasm, liked a good joke, and became a popular broadcaster after retiring even though he frequently mispronounced players' names.

Satchel Paige

A star righthanded pitcher in the Negro leagues for the Kansas City Monarchs, Paige brought his heat — and his unforgettable outlook on life — to the majors in 1948 and helped the Cleveland Indians win the pennant. "Don't look back. Something might be gaining on you," said Paige, who was elected to the Hall of Fame in '71.

Yogi Berra

Looking back, it seems as if every time Berra opened his mouth, he said something memorable. He made sense or he didn't, but today the catcher, who was a three-time MVP and a 15-time All-Star with the New York Yankees in the 1940s, '50s, and '60s, is the most quoted player in the game because of gems like, "When you come to a fork in the road, take it." And, "Nobody goes there anymore. It's too crowded."

The Merry Pranksters

⊨ 1960s ⊨
Moe Drabowsky
It takes skill to be able to set unsuspecting teammates' shoelaces on fire — known as giving a hot foot — but this sneaky relief pitcher gave one to the commissioner of baseball! The Prince of Pranks also slipped sneezing powder into opposing teams' air-conditioning systems, hid python snakes in teammates' shoes and lockers, made crank calls from the bullpen, and set off fireworks in the clubhouse bathroom.

⊨ 1970s ⊨
Jay Johnstone
Johnstone once put a soggy brownie in a teammate's glove, then tried to place the blame elsewhere by smearing fudge frosting on another teammate's uniform. He cut holes in players' underwear, nailed cleats to the floor, put pine tar in shoes, and he once locked L.A. Dodgers manager Tommy Lasorda in his office during spring training and removed the receiver from the phone so Lasorda couldn't call for help.

⊨ 1990s ⊨
Roger McDowell
The relief pitcher got so bored during a game that he put his uniform on upside down, with his pants on his head and his shirt on his legs. McDowell, also a master of the hot foot, once had a clubhouse attendant call Philadelphia Phillies teammate Tommy Greene pretending to be the prime minister of Canada after Greene pitched a no-hitter against the Montreal Expos.

⊨ 2000s ⊨
Manny Ramirez
How was this unique outfielder's behavior explained? It was just *Manny being Manny.* While playing for the Red Sox, he sneaked behind the famed Green Monster wall for a bathroom break during a pitching change and returned to the field as the new guy on the mound released his first pitch. Another time he high-fived a fan after catching a fly ball and climbing up the outfield wall — and didn't miss a beat on the throw.

⊨ 2010s ⊨
Mike Scioscia
An All-Star catcher for the L.A. Dodgers, Scioscia became a lot more creative when he took the job as the Anaheim Angels' manager. He's at his best during spring training. That's when he made pitcher John Lackey take an algebra test after he found out Lackey failed the course in junior college, made pitchers construct a fielder's glove and catcher's mitt from scratch, and sent shy rookies to interview Phoenix Suns cheerleaders.

MILESTONES

Here's an easy way to guarantee baseball immortality: Achieve one of these nice, round numbers in your career

300 Wins

	Year of 300th	Total wins
Pud Galvin	1888	365 ▷
Mickey Welch	1890	307
Tim Keefe	1890	342
Charles Radbourn	1891	309
John Clarkson	1892	328
Kid Nichols	1900	361
Cy Young	1901	511
Christy Mathewson	1912	373
Eddie Plank	1915	326
Walter Johnson	1920	417
Grover Cleveland Alexander	1924	373
Lefty Grove	1941	300
Warren Spahn	1961	363
Early Wynn	1963	300
Gaylord Perry	1982	314
Steve Carlton	1983	329
Phil Niekro	1985	318
Tom Seaver	1985	311
Don Sutton	1986	324
Nolan Ryan	1990	324
Roger Clemens	2003	354
Greg Maddux	2004	355
Tom Glavine	2007	305
Randy Johnson	2009	303 ▷

3,000 Strikeouts

	Year of 3,000th	Total strikeouts
Walter Johnson	1923	3,508 ▷
Bob Gibson	1974	3,117
Gaylord Perry	1978	3,534
Nolan Ryan	1980	5,714
Steve Carlton	1981	4,136
Tom Seaver	1981	3,640
Fergie Jenkins	1982	3,192
Don Sutton	1983	3,574
Phil Niekro	1984	3,342
Bert Blyleven	1986	3,701
Roger Clemens	1998	4,672
Randy Johnson	2000	4,875
Greg Maddux	2005	3,371
Curt Schilling	2006	3,116
Pedro Martinez	2007	3,154
John Smoltz	2008	3,084 ▷

THEN

NOW

THEN

NOW

500 Home Runs

	Year of 500th	Total home runs
Babe Ruth	1929	714 ▷
Jimmie Foxx	1940	534
Mel Ott	1945	511
Ted Williams	1960	521
Willie Mays	1965	660
Mickey Mantle	1967	536
Eddie Mathews	1967	512
Hank Aaron	1968	755
Ernie Banks	1970	512
Frank Robinson	1971	586
Harmon Killebrew	1971	573
Willie McCovey	1978	521
Reggie Jackson	1984	563
Mike Schmidt	1987	548
Eddie Murray	1996	504
Mark McGwire	1999	583
Barry Bonds	2001	762
Sammy Sosa	2003	609
Rafael Palmeiro	2003	569
Ken Griffey Jr.	2004	630
Jim Thome	2007	612
Alex Rodriguez*	2007	687
Frank Thomas	2007	521
Manny Ramirez	2008	555
Gary Sheffield	2009	509
Albert Pujols*	2014	560 ▷

THEN

NOW

*Active player

3,000 Hits

	Year of 3,000th	Total hits
Cap Anson	1897	3,418 ▷
Honus Wagner	1914	3,415
Nap Lajoie	1914	3,242
Ty Cobb	1921	4,191
Tris Speaker	1925	3,514
Eddie Collins	1925	3,315
Paul Waner	1942	3,152
Stan Musial	1958	3,630
Hank Aaron	1970	3,771
Willie Mays	1970	3,283
Roberto Clemente	1972	3,000
Al Kaline	1974	3,007
Pete Rose	1978	4,256
Lou Brock	1979	3,023
Carl Yastrzemski	1979	3,419
Rod Carew	1985	3,053
Robin Yount	1992	3,142
George Brett	1992	3,154
Dave Winfield	1993	3,110
Eddie Murray	1995	3,255
Paul Molitor	1996	3,319
Tony Gwynn	1999	3,141
Wade Boggs	1999	3,010
Cal Ripken Jr.	2000	3,184
Rickey Henderson	2001	3,055
Rafael Palmeiro	2005	3,020
Craig Biggio	2007	3,060
Derek Jeter	2011	3,465
Alex Rodriguez*	2015	3,070 ▷

THEN

NOW

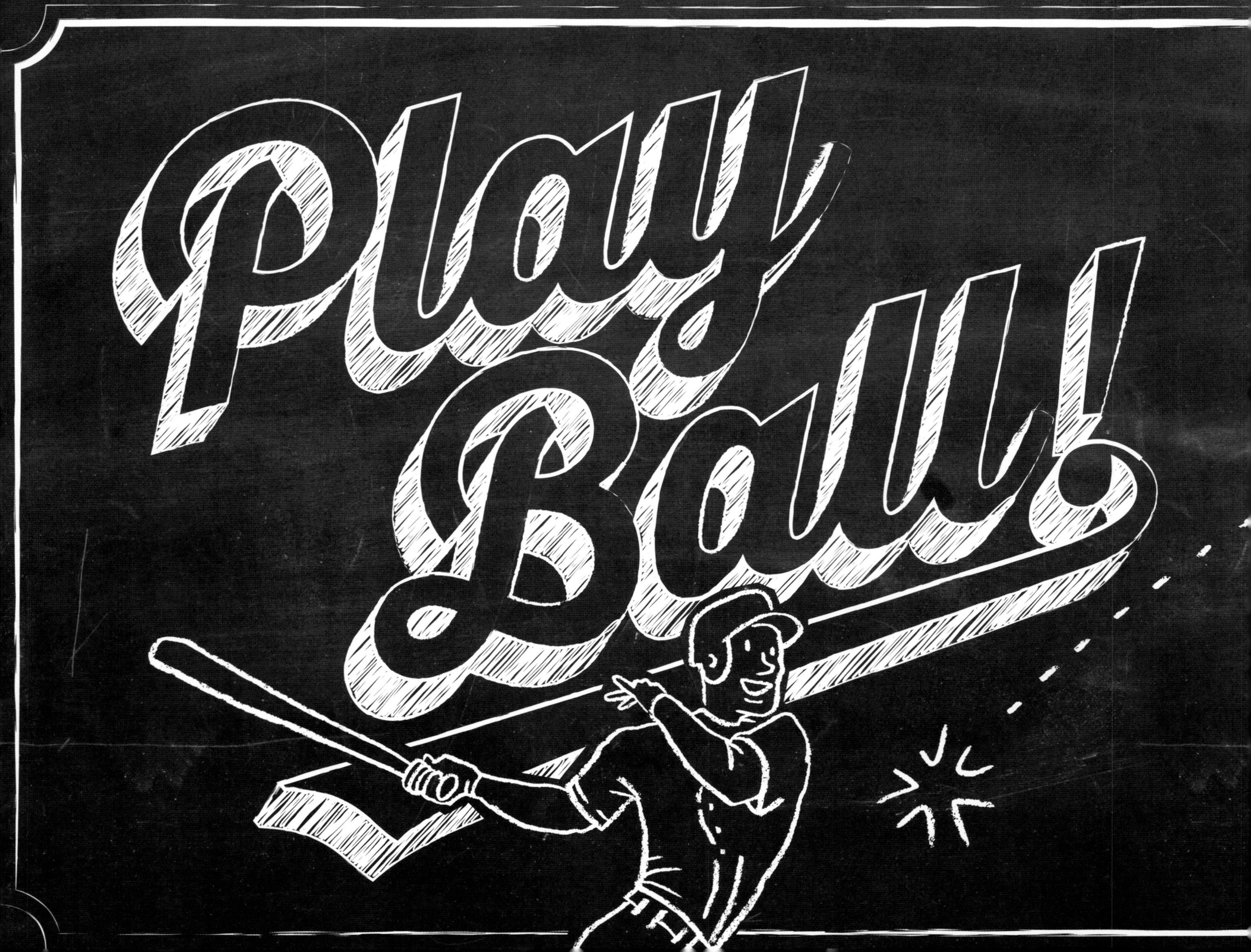
Play Ball!

O.K. The nine best players are in the lineup. Now what? From getting hitters on base, to deciding which pitchers to use in which situations, to figuring out how to build a dominant club, baseball has always been about strategy.

Successful managers — whether coaching in the minor leagues, the Negro leagues, the All-American Girls Professional Baseball League, or the majors — have adopted varying styles to motivate players. (Sometimes yelling does the trick; sometimes it gets you into trouble with the ump.) Through the years, the aim has remained the same: win!

Joe McCarthy
Cubs, Yankees, Red Sox
A quiet and thoughtful teacher, McCarthy got the most out of his players year in and year out. In 24 years, he never had a losing season, and he won seven world titles with the Yankees.

Walter Alston
Dodgers

Casey Stengel
Dodgers, Braves, Yankees, Mets

Tommy Lasorda
Dodgers

Sparky Anderson
Reds, Tigers

Dick Williams
Red Sox, A's, Angels, Expos, Padres, Mariners

Gene Mauch
Phillies, Expos, Twins, Angels

Ralph Houk
Yankees, Tigers, Red Sox

THE SILENT TYPE

Bucky Harris
Senators, Tigers, Red Sox, Phillies, Yankees

Connie Mack
Pirates, A's
Always a gentleman, Mack was thrown out just once in 53 years as a manager. He won five World Series but also had a sub-.500 winning percentage and finished last 17 times.

MANAGERS

The dugout masters who call the shots have employed a variety of styles

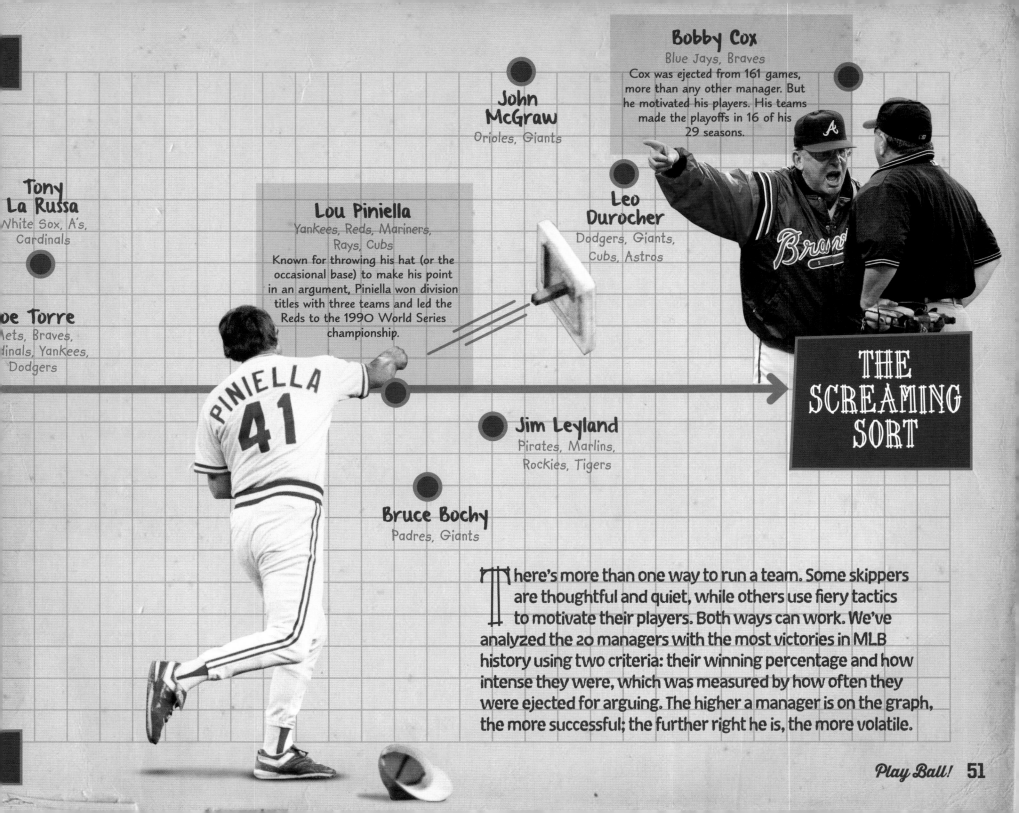

Bobby Cox
Blue Jays, Braves
Cox was ejected from 161 games, more than any other manager. But he motivated his players. His teams made the playoffs in 16 of his 29 seasons.

John McGraw
Orioles, Giants

Tony La Russa
White Sox, A's, Cardinals

Lou Piniella
Yankees, Reds, Mariners, Rays, Cubs
Known for throwing his hat (or the occasional base) to make his point in an argument, Piniella won division titles with three teams and led the Reds to the 1990 World Series championship.

Leo Durocher
Dodgers, Giants, Cubs, Astros

oe Torre
Mets, Braves,
dinals, Yankees,
Dodgers

PINIELLA 41

Jim Leyland
Pirates, Marlins, Rockies, Tigers

THE SCREAMING SORT

Bruce Bochy
Padres, Giants

There's more than one way to run a team. Some skippers are thoughtful and quiet, while others use fiery tactics to motivate their players. Both ways can work. We've analyzed the 20 managers with the most victories in MLB history using two criteria: their winning percentage and how intense they were, which was measured by how often they were ejected for arguing. The higher a manager is on the graph, the more successful; the further right he is, the more volatile.

PITCHING STAFF

Gone are the days when the same hurler would take the mound day after day after day. Pitching has become a highly specialized art

In 1884, the Providence Grays of the National League played 112 games. Charles (Old Hoss) Radbourn was practically a one-man staff: He started 73 games — and completed every single one of them. By comparison, in 2014, no pitcher had more than 34 starts or six complete games. Teams often carry up to 12 pitchers on their 25-man rosters, and each one has a specific duty. If Radbourn pitched today, the hardest adjustment he'd have to make would be finding a way to fill all of his spare time!

Pitcher

THEN

⇒ 1900s ⇒ 10s ⇒

In the early days of baseball, home runs were rare. One reason was that balls were seldom taken out of play, and the longer they were used, the softer they became. In the so-called Dead Ball era, managers had to "manufacture" runs by frequently bunting to advance runners and by stealing bases. Then, in 1919, Babe Ruth bashed 29 home runs, showing the value of power hitters. Players were encouraged to swing for the fences, and run production began to boom.

To bunt or not to bunt? Managers have used many methods to find success on the field

⇒ 1940s ⇒
Platoon System

Since it is easier for a batter to hit a ball that is breaking toward him, righthanded hitters tend to have more success against lefthanded pitchers. (And the opposite is true: Lefty hitters do better against righty pitchers.) In the 1940s, New York Yankees manager Casey Stengel popularized the strategy of changing his lineup depending on the pitcher. He basically had two groups of hitters, or "platoons." The righthanded group played against lefthanded pitchers. And when a righty was on the mound, more lefties batted. (Stengel didn't platoon at every position: He'd want a slugger like Yogi Berra in the lineup no matter who was on the hill.) One of the Yankees' better-known platoons was at first base. In 1956, Moose Skowron *(near right)* and Joe Collins *(far right)* split time, combining for 30 homers and 133 RBIs as the Yankees won the World Series.

STRATEGIES

⇒ 1960s ⇐
The Earl of the Dugout

In 1968, the Baltimore Orioles hired Earl Weaver as their manager. Weaver had a simple game plan: rely on pitching and home runs. He hated sacrifice bunts and stolen bases because they risked wasting outs. With aces like Jim Palmer *(below, left)* and sluggers such as Boog Powell *(below, right)*, Weaver's teams made the playoffs five times between 1969 and '74. Weaver was also one of the first managers to make lineup decisions based on how a hitter fared against a certain pitcher in the past, often leaving Powell on the bench if he was supposed to face a pitcher he struggled against.

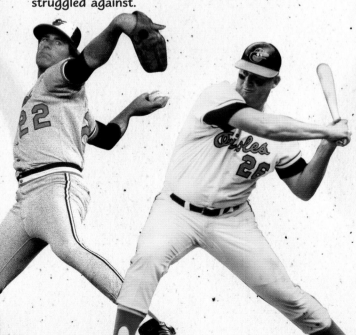

⇒ 1970s⇒80s ⇐
Whiteyball

In 1977, 10 of the 26 stadiums in the majors had artificial turf, and many had spacious outfields. Several teams adopted a strategy of using fast players who could slap the ball on the turf and beat out hits. Manager Whitey Herzog won three division titles with the Kansas City Royals in the late '70s with speedy lineups that were low on power, but his '82 St. Louis Cardinals team was the ultimate Whiteyball squad. The Cards hit just 67 home runs (that's three fewer than Cardinal Mark McGwire hit by himself in '98), but they stole 200 bases — 35 more than any other team in the league. Led by rookie Willie McGee *(above)*, St. Louis beat the slugging Milwaukee Brewers in the World Series.

⇒ Today ⇐
Moneyball

As salaries escalated in the 2000s, teams that couldn't afford to pay superstars had to find other ways to become competitive. The Oakland A's were known for this; their brand of baseball was called Moneyball. Since they couldn't outspend their foes, they tried to outthink them. The A's pioneered the use of advanced statistical analysis to make personnel and game-strategy decisions. (For instance, the Moneyball philosophy doesn't encourage bunting, because analysis showed that sacrificing outs wasn't beneficial enough.) The shift toward the use of advanced stats has changed the way many teams are run. In the past, general managers tended to be former players or coaches. Now, many are business or law school graduates.

UMPIRES

Nobody loves the ump. It's true. But these oft-berated officials have always upheld the rules, even if they don't look as stylish as they once did

Four-men crews were used in World Series games beginning in 1909, but it wasn't until '52 that four umpires worked every regular-season matchup. Six-men crews have been used for Series games since '47.

Until 1912, umpires like Charles Daniels (*right*) worked alone — and without much equipment standing between them and the ball. Daniels is thought to be the first ump to wear shin guards.

Chest protectors came into vogue in 1885. Six years later Tom Connolly (*right*), one of 10 men in blue in the Hall of Fame, umpired the first American League game.

1880s

1900s

1960s

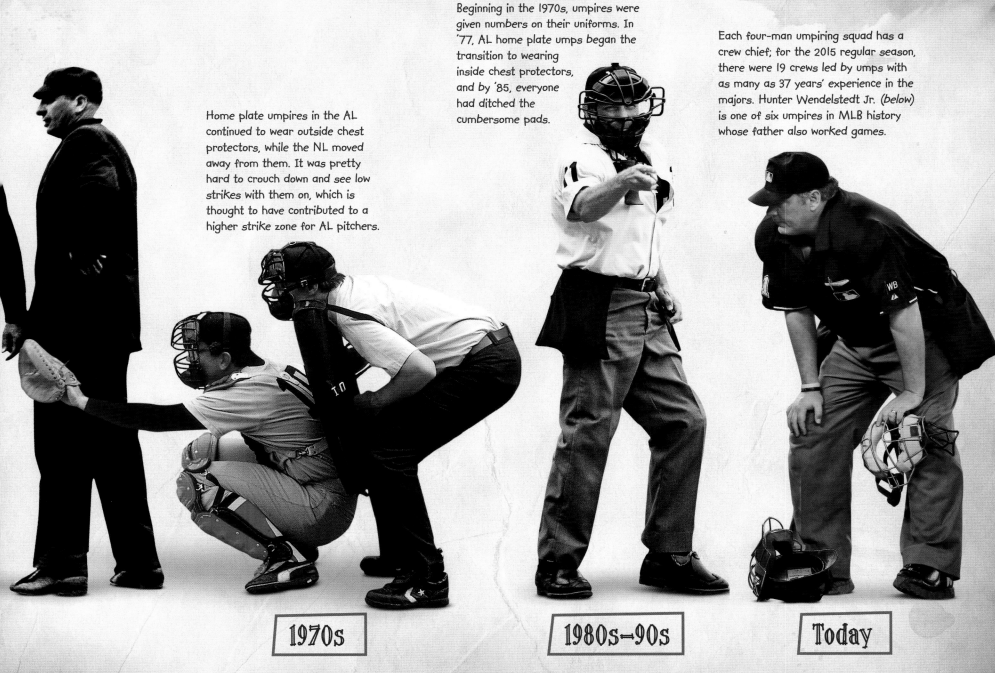

Home plate umpires in the AL continued to wear outside chest protectors, while the NL moved away from them. It was pretty hard to crouch down and see low strikes with them on, which is thought to have contributed to a higher strike zone for AL pitchers.

Beginning in the 1970s, umpires were given numbers on their uniforms. In '77, AL home plate umps began the transition to wearing inside chest protectors, and by '85, everyone had ditched the cumbersome pads.

Each four-man umpiring squad has a crew chief; for the 2015 regular season, there were 19 crews led by umps with as many as 37 years' experience in the majors. Hunter Wendelstedt Jr. (*below*) is one of six umpires in MLB history whose father also worked games.

1970s

1980s–90s

Today

MINOR LEAGUES

1901 to TODAY

The minor leagues, formally organized in 1901, develop talent and provide a place for players recovering from injury to regain their form before heading back to the majors. Players are "called up" to the big leagues when they have proved themselves and are sent back down if they need more work.

~ 1921 ~
Major league teams were now allowed to own minor league teams. St. Louis Cardinals manager and GM Branch Rickey essentially created the farm system that we know today, which allows organizations to cultivate their own talent.

~ 1933 ~
Playing for the Double A San Francisco Seals, future Yankees Hall of Famer Joe DiMaggio had a 61-game hitting streak, five games longer than the major league record of 56 he would set in 1941.

ALL-AMERICAN GIRLS PROFESSIONAL BASEBALL LEAGUE

1920 to 1960

With many of the country's major and minor league baseball players fighting in World War II, Chicago Cubs owner Philip K. Wrigley had the idea to start a women's league. The final tryouts — for four teams located in the Midwest — were held at Wrigley Field in 1943. After the war, the league expanded to as many as 10 teams before folding after the '54 season.

NOT JUST A MAN'S GAME
Players — such as the 1953 Fort Wayne (Indiana) Daisies *(left)* — were held to much higher standards than their male counterparts in many ways and were expected to follow a handbook that included beauty routines, along with charm and etiquette guidelines.

THE NEGRO LEAGUES: HALL OF FAMERS

1943 to 1954

Because of discrimination within Major League Baseball, black players had to form their own clubs, often barnstorming (traveling around the country) to find teams to play against. The Negro leagues provided an organized way for the best African-American and Latino players to showcase their skills. Baseball was integrated in 1947, and by the mid-1960s, there were no Negro league teams left.

RUBE FOSTER
An accomplished pitcher when he was in his 20s, Foster became an owner-manager in 1911, when he was only 32. He is known as the "father of black baseball" because in 1920, he helped start the Negro National League, the first of the Negro leagues.

JOSH GIBSON
Perhaps the greatest power hitter of all time (in any league), Gibson is said to have hit a 580-foot home run. He was inducted into the Hall of Fame in 1972.

-1949-
A total of 39.7 million people attended minor league games, an all-time high.

-1954-
Joe Bauman hit 72 home runs for the Class C Roswell (New Mexico) Rockets, a professional record that stood until Barry Bonds broke it by slamming 73 dingers in 2001.

-1981-
The Pawtucket (Rhode Island) Red Sox beat the Rochester (New York) Red Wings 3–2 in 33 innings, the longest professional baseball game in history.

-1991-
The Buffalo (New York) Bisons welcomed 1,240,951 fans to their games, setting a minor league record. Every year from 1988 to '93, the team exceeded one million fans.

-2011-
Derek Jeter played to sellout crowds in Trenton, New Jersey, for the Double A Thunder while rehabbing a calf injury.

ALWAYS PEACHY
Dorothy Kamenshek starred for the Rockford (Illinois) Peaches for 10 seasons.

LEAGUES of their OWN

Sure, the big leagues are a big deal, but talented baseball players have flourished over the last century in organizations other than Major League Baseball

JAMES (COOL PAPA) BELL
Bell was so fast, as roommate Josh Gibson liked to say, he could switch off the light and be in bed before the room went dark. Bell, a switch-hitter, played in 11 All-Star Games and had a 341 batting average over his career.

1936 CRAWFORDS
The Pittsburgh powerhouse team boasted Bell *(seventh from right)*, Gibson *(fourth from right)*, and fellow Hall of Famer Satchel Paige *(second from right)*.

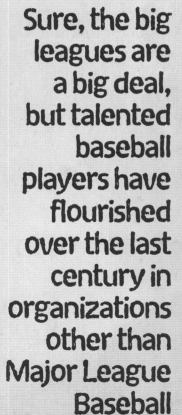

DYNASTIES: *The Yankees*

In winning 27 world championships, more than any other team, the New York Yankees have had several periods of pure dominance

1920s

They Could Really Kill the Ball

The 1927 lineup was so feared that the team became known as Murderers' Row. With Babe Ruth (60 home runs), Lou Gehrig (47), and Tony Lazzeri (18) supplying most of the pop, the Yankees won 110 games and swept the Pittsburgh Pirates in the World Series. (Babe Ruth batted .400 in those four games.) Add Bob Meusel to the list and you had four players with more than 100 RBIs each. Leadoff hitter Earle Combs led the AL in hits (231) and triples (23).

AL CHAMPIONS

1926 1927 1928

1930s

The Bronx Bombers Are Really Born

As the United States struggled through a time of economic depression, the Yankees were enjoying a period of prosperity never before seen in modern baseball. Babe Ruth had already retired, but manager Joe McCarthy's lineup still packed plenty of punch: Hall of Famers Lou Gehrig *(above, far left)*, Joe DiMaggio, and Bill Dickey combined for 354 home runs over those four seasons to help the Yanks outslug all MLB teams by nearly 200 dingers during that time.

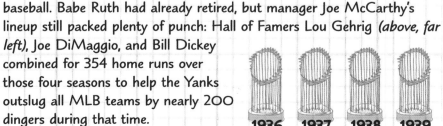

1936 1937 1938 1939

1950s

Perfect? Just About

No team has ever matched New York's streak of five consecutive World Series wins. In fact, other than the 1930s Yankees, no team has won more than three in a row. Beginning with manager Casey Stengel's first year at the helm, the Yankees were simply dominant. One of the many highlights was pitcher Don Larsen's perfect game that put the Yanks up 3–2 in the '56 Series against the crosstown-rival Brooklyn Dodgers. (That's Larsen embracing catcher Yogi Berra, *above*.)

1949 1950 1951 1952 1953 1955 1956 1957 1958

1990s

Plenty of Pinstripe Victories

The year Joe Torre became the team's manager, he led them to a 4–2 World Series win over the Atlanta Braves. As it turned out, the Yanks were just getting started. All-Star-studded starting lineups included Bernie Williams in centerfield, Derek Jeter at shortstop, Paul O'Neill in rightfield, and Tino Martinez at first base. And what pitching staffs the Yankees put together! Aces David Cone, Roger Clemens, Andy Pettitte, and David Wells all earned rings, as did super closers Mariano Rivera and John Wetteland (*above*, pointing).

1996 1998 1999 2000

DYNASTIES: The Rest

The Yankees didn't corner the market on success *every* year. These teams enjoyed extended seasons in the spotlight

1880s

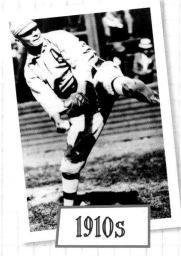

1910s

1920s

St. Louis Browns

These Browns may have played more than a century before you were born, but they owned the young American Association. Future Hall of Fame executive Charles Comiskey was an infielder for the Browns and also became the team's manager in 1883, when he was only 24 years old.

1885   1886   1887   1888

Philadelphia Athletics

Stoic manager Connie Mack presided over nine AL champions during the 50 years he led the A's. Five of those teams — including the 1910 and '11 clubs that won the Series with help from Hall of Fame ace Chief Bender *(above)* — won more than 100 games.

1910   1911   1913   1914

New York Giants

Another New York team did all right in the early 20th century too. Hall of Fame manager John McGraw, who had lost three straight championships from 1911 through '13, led the Giants to back-to-back wins a decade later. The victories were especially sweet: The Giants beat Babe Ruth and the Yankees both times.

1921   1922   1923   1924

1940s

St. Louis Cardinals

Stan (the Man) Musial *(above, second from left)* and Enos (Country) Slaughter *(far left)* helped drive this Midwest machine despite missing time in the 1940s while serving in the U.S. military. Slaughter's famed Mad Dash clinched Game 7 of the '46 Series against the Boston Red Sox: With the score tied 3–3 in the eighth, he scored from first base on a hit to center.

1950s

Brooklyn/L.A. Dodgers

They endured heartbreak at the hands of the other two New York teams of the era (the Yankees and the Giants), but the Dodgers finally broke through in 1955 thanks to stars such as Pee Wee Reese, Jackie Robinson *(above)*, and Roy Campanella. The club packed up and moved to Los Angeles before the '58 season and won the Series the next year. Perpetual All-Star Gil Hodges and Hall of Famer Duke Snider were members of both world championship teams.

1970s

Oakland A's

Apparently, in the 1970s, the more mustaches you had on your team, the more championship rings you got. The A's sported the finest bunch of facial hair you've ever seen — and they were also really, really good at baseball. Reggie Jackson, Gene Tenace *(above, center)*, and Sal Bando led the way offensively, while Catfish Hunter and Rollie Fingers (who maintained the ultimate handlebar mustache) were masters on the mound.

2010s

San Francisco Giants

With their 2014 Series win, the Giants, who also moved from New York to the West Coast in 1958, became the second NL team (after the '40s Cardinals) to ever win three championships over a span of five years. Starting pitcher Madison Bumgarner *(above, right, with catcher Buster Posey)* was a hero in the 2014 Game 7 clincher against the Kansas City Royals, tossing five scoreless innings in relief three nights after a nine-inning win.

1942 1943 1944 1946

1952 1953 1955 1956 1959

1972 1973 1974

2010 2012 2014

Over the years, baseball has become more and more about keeping spectators entertained and engaged. A candy bar with Babe Ruth's name on the wrapper? *I'd buy that!* Trading cards with pictures of the game's most beloved players? *I want a pack!* A free bat just for walking through the gate? *Well, duh!* Today's fans can have Cracker Jack *and* sushi while they sit in the stands and enjoy nine innings of fun.

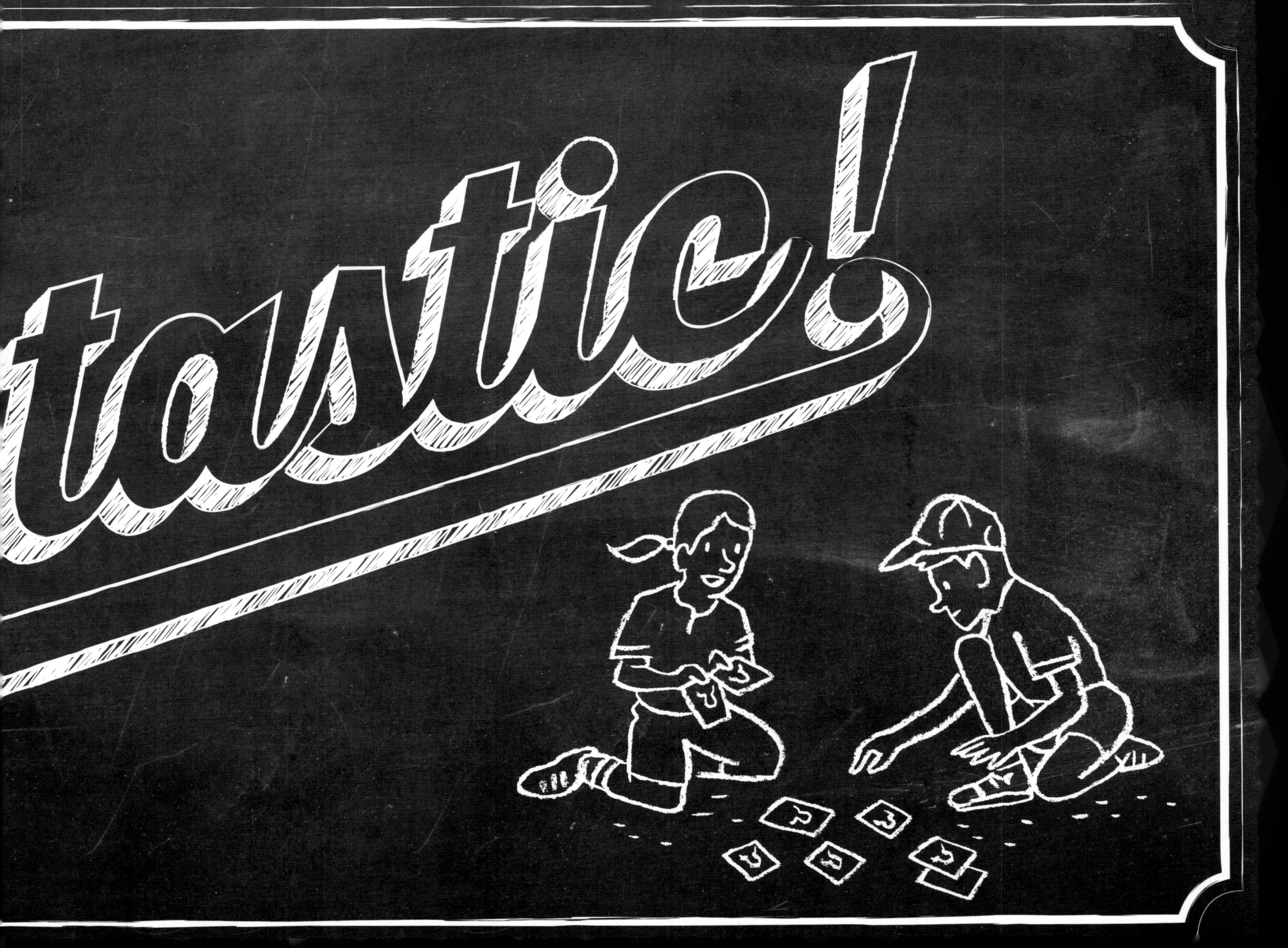
tastic!

The NAME GAME

How do you know you're famous? When you have a candy bar named after you. Or a breakfast cereal, or a soft drink . . .

= 1926 =
Babe Ruth's Candy Bar

Those were the days, right? A nickel would buy you a candy bar with the Babe himself on the wrapper. These were different than Baby Ruth bars, which debuted in 1921 and were *not*, the company that manufactured them maintained, named for the Yankees' slugger. That company sued to get this bar off the shelves in '31 — and won. Baby Ruths are still around today.

= 1960s =
Ted Williams's Fishing Equipment

Williams frequently used his free time during Red Sox spring training in Florida to fish. He loved the sport and even wrote a book about it: *Fishing the Big Three: Tarpon, Bonefish, Atlantic Salmon.* He's in the Baseball Hall of Fame *and* the International Game Fish Association Hall of Fame.

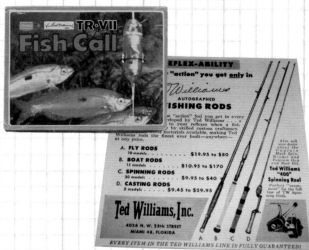

= 1960s =
Rocky Colavito's Dart Game

Colavito was told he had been traded from the Cleveland Indians to the Detroit Tigers while standing on first base during an exhibition game in the spring of 1960. Who knows? Maybe he got out some of his anger while playing this dart game, which made its debut after the trade.

= circa 1978 =
Lou Brock's Soda Pop

One of the sport's speediest (he's second on the all-time steals list) endorsed this cherry-flavored soda while with the St. Louis Cardinals.

≈ 1978 ≈
Reggie Jackson's Candy Bar

"If I played in New York, they'd name a candy bar after me," Jackson said while playing for the Oakland A's. He did, and they did. The Yankees gave away this treat at the 1978 home opener. Jackson hit a home run, prompting fans to throw the candy onto the field.

≈ 1991 ≈
Bo Jackson's Kicks

A college football star as a running back at Auburn University in the early 1980s, Jackson was selected in the NFL *and* MLB drafts. He played football for the Oakland Raiders for four years and wore a baseball uniform for the Royals, White Sox, and Angels over an eight-year MLB career. Nike's Air Trainers — which Jackson made a sensation with his "Bo Knows" ads — are still sold today, usually with details that pay homage to the talented athlete, who was also a state champion track star in high school.

≈ 1998 ≈
Omar Vizquel's Salsa

Vizquel was in the middle of his first All-Star and sixth straight Gold Glove season when this product hit the market in Cleveland. The Indians' shortstop was so popular that fans had bought 100,000 jars of salsa within the first three months it was in stores.

≈ 1999 ≈
Sammy Sosa's Cereal

The summer after Sosa won NL MVP and raced Mark McGwire for the single-season home run record, Famous Fixins sold $1 million worth of these frosted flakes. Sosa had hit 66 round-trippers and McGwire had hit 70, both of which beat Yankee Roger Maris's mark of 61.

≈ 2012 ≈
Joey Votto's Cereal

M-V-P! M-V-P! TOAST-ED OATS? Yes, you could buy this breakfast food in and around Cincinnati to celebrate the Reds' first baseman, who won the NL's top award in 2010.

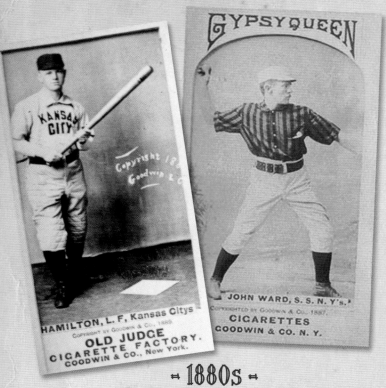

⊨ 1880s ⊨
Tobacco is King

Baseball was increasing in popularity in the United States, and in 1875, tobacco companies began including cards on the back of their cigarette boxes. Soon companies were numbering cards as part of a set in the hope that smokers would want to collect all 25 or 50 cards — and especially that kids would ask their parents to buy certain brands based on the cards they wanted.

⊨ 1900s ⊨
The Frenzy Begins

The American Tobacco Company began putting cards into their cigarette packages in 1909. To youngsters in the U.S., as the *Charlotte Observer* wrote that year, these were "more sought after than gold." Pittsburgh Pirates star Honus Wagner's card was part of the company's T206 set. (In 2013, one of these cards sold for $2.1 million!) Wanting to capitalize on the appeal the cards held for consumers, other companies began offering cards with their products too.

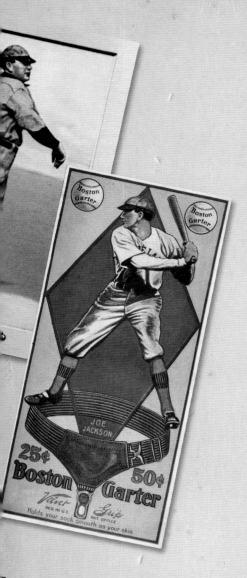

GEORGE HERMAN
(BABE) RUTH

BIG LEAGUE CHEWING GUM

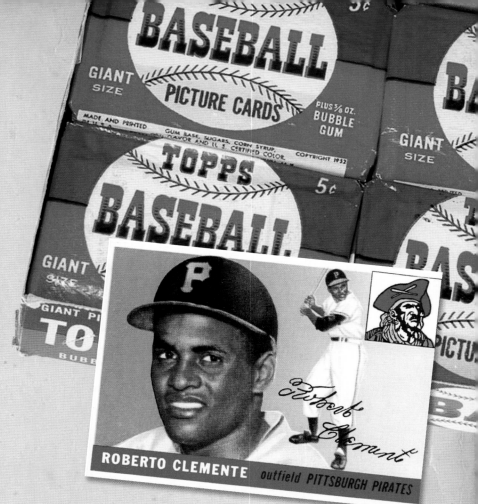

BASEBALL PICTURE CARDS

GIANT SIZE

PLUS ⅙ OZ. BUBBLE GUM

TOPPS BASEBALL 5¢

ROBERTO CLEMENTE outfield PITTSBURGH PIRATES

⇥ 1930s ⇤
Bubble Time

Finally, cards that kids could buy with their allowance money! Fleer included cards with candy, and Goudey, which manufactured gum, included much better looking cards — such as Babe Ruth's *(above)*, part of a 240-card set — that kids went nuts over in 1933. Goudey released multiple cards that featured the same player, another ploy to entice kids to want to collect within that set.

⇥ 1950s ⇤
Topps Enters the Picture

Topps Chewing Gum was founded in 1938, and 10 years later, the company began selling packs with cards. In '51, Topps released its first series — each pack came with taffy — meant to be used to play "card-baseball." The following year, the company produced its first annual trading card set. Packs *(top)* had wax wrappers and included six cards and a stick of gum for five cents. Future Hall of Famer Roberto Clemente's '55 rookie card *(above)* had a trivia question on the back.

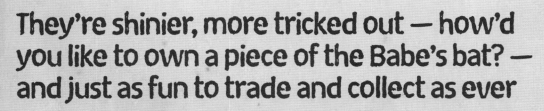

They're shinier, more tricked out — how'd you like to own a piece of the Babe's bat? — and just as fun to trade and collect as ever

FLEER

Kirby Puckett
OUTFIELD

SELECT CERTIFIED EDITION

Derek Jeter

'96
Rookie

ROGER MARIS

MICKEY MANTLE

GAME-USED BAT

BABE RUTH

GAME-WORN PANTS

ROGER MARIS

GAME-WORN PANTS

FIVE STAR
08/10

CHASE '61

Topps Heritage

$15

WORL TRIBUT
October 1, 1932

BABE R

SS

UPPER DECK 90

CINCINNATI REDS

Barry Larkin

MAJOR LEAGUE
BASEBALL
The COLLECTOR'S Choice
3-D TEAM LOGO HOLOGRAMS AND BASEBALL CARDS
1989

A Minimum of One 3-D Team Logo Hologram per pack!
Limited Edition, High Quality Cards
15 Baseball Cards per pack
Counterfeit-Proof Cards
Random Sequencing
Tamper-Proof Pack

WIN!

A Minimum of One 3-D Team Logo Hologram & 15 Baseball Cards

⋍1970s⋍90s⋍
Foiled for the First Time

Topps essentially owned the market until the mid-1970s, when Fleer took the company to court for controlling too much of the industry. (Topps had contracts with just about every MLB player.) Upper Deck came into the picture in '89, revolutionizing the way cards were manufactured and authenticated. The glossy cards were wrapped in foil and included holograms on the back that made the cards more difficult to illegally copy.

⋍2000s⋍
Scraps and Bats

As kids became interested in other pastimes — video games! — companies tried to find ways to keep youngsters, and also adult collectors, interested in trading cards. In the late 1990s, companies began inserting pieces of current players' uniforms and bats into the cards. Donruss paid more than $250,000 in 2003 for one of Babe Ruth's 1925 game-worn jerseys, then cut it up into 2,100 pieces. Many diehard fans and collectors disagreed with this, especially since the jersey was only one of three thought to be in existence.

= 2009 =
How'd They Do That?

No, players didn't really pop up out of the cards that Topps produced in '09, but held in front of a webcam, they came to life on your screen, and you could make them swing, pitch, or shag a fly ball.

TODAY

In 2009, Topps received exclusive rights from MLB to print cards with league logos on them, a deal that has been extended until at least '20. Other companies, such as Upper Deck, can still produce cards with players' images on them, but they can't use the logos.

⋆ 1860s ⋆

The first baseball board games began appearing before baseball was even a professional sport. Most were fairly simple by today's standards. Usually cards, dice, or spinners randomly determined the outcome.

⋆ 1940s ⋆

All-Star Baseball, which debuted in 1941, was one of the first games to feature actual players. Baseball stars were represented by round cards. The game player spun a dial, which pointed to a result on the hitter's disc. Eventually new games — such as Strat-o-Matic Baseball — were based even more on statistics, offering realistic results.

Not every baseball contest takes place on a diamond using a bat and ball. Gamers have been simulating the national pastime for nearly a century and a half

GAME TIME

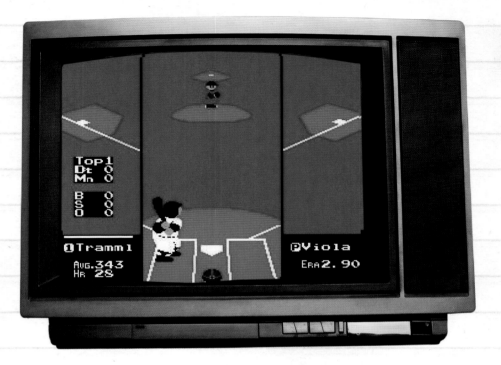

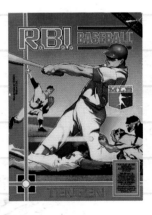

⇢ 1980s ⇠

Baseball video games began to appear in the 1970s, but the first one to feature MLB players was *R.B.I. Baseball*. What it lacked in graphics, it made up for in novelty: The '86 release allowed gamers to be their favorite major league stars. *R.B.I.* took into account players' strengths and weaknesses. So a flamethrower like Roger Clemens or Nolan Ryan was especially hard to hit. Of course, today's video games have taken realism to a whole new level. *MLB 15: The Show*, for instance, features announcers and players who look so much like their real-life counterparts that it's easy to confuse watching a video game with watching an actual game!

⇢ Today ⇠

Much like baseball itself, fantasy baseball has murky origins. Several groups take credit for inventing the game. The earliest versions date to the 1970s and '80s, when league statistics had to be tallied by hand. Most fantasy leagues at that point featured eight statistical categories: four on offense (batting average, home runs, RBIs, and stolen bases) and four pitching (wins, saves, ERA, and WHIP). The game gradually grew in popularity, and with the advent of the Internet, it took off in the late '90s. Now nearly 20 million people play fantasy baseball in leagues featuring several formats. There are even daily fantasy leagues that allow players to draft entirely new squads every day.

YOU'RE UP!

You don't have to be a major leaguer to play

T-ball
The game that allows beginners to get used to hitting without having to face a pitcher debuted in the 1950s. Now, more than two million aspiring sluggers play T-ball.

Stickball
Kids were playing stick-and-ball games long before baseball was invented. The most popular do-it-yourself game is probably stickball. Rules vary by location, but the basics are the same: A rubber ball (or sometimes a tennis ball) is pitched to a batter, who tries to hit it with a bat-like piece of wood, often a broom handle. Bases can be anything from a hat to a manhole cover to a spot on the curb.

Little League
Founded by Carl Stotz in 1939, Little League Baseball originally featured just three teams. The games were played in a vacant lot in Stotz's hometown of Williamsport, Pennsylvania. Little League expanded outside the state in '47.

Wiffle Ball

The plastic ball that darts and dips all over the place has been a staple of backyard games since it was invented in the 1950s. The oblong holes on one half of the ball allow pitchers to throw wicked curves, while the ball's lightweight plastic construction means that it is safe — for players as well as windows!

Softball

More popular with girls than boys, softball is played with a larger ball than baseball. In 1969 the first Women's College World Series was held, and from '96 through 2008 women's softball was an Olympic sport.

Little League World Series

It's safe to say that Little League has grown from the small operation Carl Stotz founded. Every year, 2.4 million players in all 50 states and more than 80 countries play Little League. In August, the top 10- to 12-year-olds descend on South Williamsport, Pennsylvania, for the World Series. Sixteen teams (eight from the U.S. and eight international) compete over 10 days in front of crowds that can exceed 40,000 fans.

GAME DAY

Not that you need another incentive to head to the ballpark, but isn't it fun to get a little something extra?

Bat Day

For this event, the Texas Rangers typically prepare around 65,000 hot dogs. By 2015, there were 11 such promotions on the Rangers' schedule. That's a lot of dogs!

Dollar Dog Night

The St. Louis Browns handed out bats at a Father's Day doubleheader.

Ladies' Day

1948

1952

1990s

Master promoter Bill Veeck gave away livestock to some lucky Cleveland Indians fans.

1940s

The promotion came and went throughout the first half of the 20th century, with clubs often admitting women for free or at a discounted price, especially to weekday games.

1960s

These yes-men really took off in the 1960s, when players like Mickey Mantle were immortalized as toys. By 2015, nearly every team had at least one bobblehead giveaway.

PERKS

The L.A. Dodgers gave away baseballs. Maybe not the best idea. Fans threw them onto the field at multiple points during the game, including after batter Raul Mondesi and manager Tommy Lasorda were ejected for arguing a call. The Dodgers, down 2–1 in the ninth to the St. Louis Cardinals, had to forfeit!

1995

Buzz Cut Night

For a free ticket to see the Seattle Mariners on Buhner Buzz Cut Night, all you had to do was make a charitable donation and show off your bald head — or get it shaved outside the stadium, maybe even by Jay Buhner, the popular rightfielder for whom the promotion was named.

1997

In honor of Wrigley Field's 100th anniversary, the Cubs did decade-by-decade throwback giveaways, including for this toy that debuted in the 1960s.

2014

1997

The Beanie Baby craze made it to MLB ballparks. During a game in 1998, the Oakland A's attracted 33,000 more fans than their average the day of their giveaway.

2006

It's fitting that the Detroit Tigers would have a car giveaway. Their hometown is called the Motor City, after all. Area Chevy dealers gave away 16 cars in 2006.

2014

How about some bling for your ring finger? Fans at Fenway Park received replicas of Boston's 2013 World Series jewelry.

2015

Tampa Bay Rays third baseman Evan Longoria as a rubber duckie? Anything is possible.

BALLPARK FOOD

To have the full game experience, you have to grab some grub. Baseball wouldn't be the same without these dishes

The most famous hot dog in baseball was born in Los Angeles when the team moved into Dodger Stadium. Thomas G. Arthur, who ran the park's concessions, had the idea to give his 10-inch hot dogs this alliterative nickname, and it stuck. Today, the Dodgers sell upward of three million hot dogs a year, around twice as many as any other major league team.

1960s

Once refrigeration became widespread in America, you could finally buy ice cream at a baseball game. What's better on a hot day in the bleachers?

1940s

Popcorn had been popular in the United States since the 19th century, and it was an easy concession to sell and eat during a game.

1930s

The most famous sports song in America made its debut in 1908. "Take Me Out To the Ball Game" described a perfect day at the park, complete with peanuts (which had been a commercial crop in America since the early 1800s), and Cracker Jack (which had been sold since the 1890s). By 1912, Cracker Jack packaging advertised "a prize in every box." Now that is something to look forward to!

1900s

Wrigley Field in Chicago sold six-inch Ron Santo pizzas. The beloved Cubs Hall of Fame third baseman opened his own pizzeria and later became an announcer for the team's radio broadcasts.

1960s

The state of Wisconsin is known for its sausages, so it wasn't too shocking when the Milwaukee Brewers started having humans dressed in meat costumes race against each other during home games. There's (from left) Hot Dog, Italian Sausage, Polish Sausage, Brat, and Chorizo. Who has your vote?

1990s

When the Baltimore Orioles opened Camden Yards in 1992, former slugger Boog Powell opened a barbecue stand at the new ballpark. The BBQ craze caught on nationwide, and Powell, even at 73 years old in 2014, was still making appearances. He has even written some cookbooks.

1990s

It's not exactly finger food, but sushi has become a hot seller at AT&T Park in San Francisco, where the Giants play. Time to be adventurous and grab some chopsticks!

2000s

Did you say you were looking for an eight-pound burger to share with seven of your friends? We thought so. Nationals Park in Washington, D.C., debuted the StrasBurger in 2012 in honor of pitcher Stephen Strasburg. It cost $59 and included a side of fries and a pitcher of soda.

2010s

79

FAST CARRY-OUT & DELIVERY SERVICE IN OUR HOT BOXES

Ron Santo Pizzeria

963-9603

PHOTO CREDITS

COVER National Baseball Hall of Fame Library, Cooperstown, NY/AP (1920s); Courtesy of Brian Interland (1940s); Hulton Archive/Getty Images (1950s); Walter Iooss Jr. for Sports Illustrated (1960s); Focus on Sport/Getty Images (1980s); John Biever for Sports Illustrated (1990s); David E. Klutho for Sports Illustrated (2000s); Jason O. Watson/Getty Images (2010s)

TITLE Robert Beck for Sports Illustrated (black bat); David N. Berkwitz for Sports Illustrated (wood bat); Milo Stewart/National Baseball Hall of Fame Library, Cooperstown, NY (Knickerbockers baseball); Rich Pilling/Getty Images (MLB baseball)

UNIFORMS Courtesy of National Past Time Museum (1860s); National Baseball Hall of Fame Library/MLB Photos/Getty Images (Boston, 1880s–90s); Underwood & Underwood/Corbis (1880s–90s, 1910s); New York Times Co./Getty Images (1900s); Hulton Archive/Getty Images (1920s); Sporting News/Rogers Photo Archive/Getty Images (1930s); Kidwiler Collection/Diamond Images/Getty Images (1950s); Bettmann/Corbis (1960s); Focus on Sport/Getty Images (Pirates); Manny Millan for Sports Illustrated (White Sox); Walter Iooss Jr. for Sports Illustrated (Indians, Orioles); Rich Pilling/MLB Photos/Getty Images (Astros); Focus on Sport/Getty Images (Cardinals); Kathy Willens/AP (Yankees); David Banks/Getty Images (Rays)

GLOVES Bret Wills for Sports Illustrated (1880s, 1900s, 1930s, 1980s, 2000s); Susan Einstein for Sports Illustrated (1890s); Milo Stewart/National Baseball Hall of Fame Library (1950s, 2010s)

MASKS Bret Wills for Sports Illustrated (1870s, 1880s, 1920s, 1940s, 1970s, 1980s); Michael Heape for Sports Illustrated (1990s); Lisa Blumenfeld/Getty Images (2010s)

STADIUMS Bettmann/Corbis (Fenway Park); Ralph Crane/The Life Picture Collection/Getty Images (Dodger Stadium); MLB Photos/Getty Images (Veterans Stadium); Judy Griesedieck/The Life Images Collection/Getty Images (Metrodome); Joe Robbins/Getty Images (Safeco Field)

SLUGGERS Bettmann/Corbis (Ruth); National Baseball Hall of Fame Library (Gehrig, Foxx); National Baseball Hall of Fame Library/MLB Photos/Getty Images (Williams); Walter Iooss Jr. for Sports Illustrated (Mays); Focus on Sport/Getty Images (Aaron, Schmidt); John Biever for Sports Illustrated (Griffey Jr.); David E. Klutho for Sports Illustrated (Pujols); Fred Vuich for Sports Illustrated (Cabrera)

FIVE-TOOL PLAYER Photo File/Getty Images (Mantle); Tom DiPace (Trout)

HIT MEN Tom DiPace for Sports Illustrated (Gwynn); Tony Triolo for Sports Illustrated (Clemente); David Liam Kyle for Sports Illustrated (Brett); John G. Zimmerman for Sports Illustrated (Carew); Herb Scharfman for Sports Illustrated (Rose); Ronald C. Modra/Sport Imagery/Getty Images (Boggs); Photo File/MLB Photos/Getty Images (Musial)

GLOVE WIZARDS John Iacono for Sports Illustrated (Bonds); Neil Leifer for Sports Illustrated (Robinson); Manny Millan for Sports Illustrated (Smith); Charles Hoff/NY Daily News Archive/Getty Images (Mays); Ronald C. Modra for Sports Illustrated (Maddux); Focus on Sport/Getty Images (Bench, Hernandez); AP (Mazeroski); Art Shay for Sports Illustrated (Clemente)

FLAMETHROWERS Transcendental Graphics/Getty Images (Johnson); AP (Feller); Focus on Sport/Getty Images (Ryan); John W. McDonough for Sports Illustrated (Chapman)

PITCH MASTERS Neil Leifer for Sports Illustrated (Koufax); Robert Beck for Sports Illustrated (Kershaw); Mike Ehrmann/Getty Images (Rivera); Victor Decolongon/Getty Images (Jansen); George Gojkovich/Getty Images (Niekro); Chuck Solomon for Sports Illustrated (Dickey); John Iacono for Sports Illustrated (Carlton); Ronald Martinez/Getty Images (Darvish); AP (Mathewson); John W. McDonough for Sports Illustrated (Hoffman); Jed Jacobsohn for Sports Illustrated (Hernandez)

SPEEDSTERS Mitchell Layton/Getty Images (Lofton); Ronald C. Modra for Sports Illustrated (Henderson); Neil Leifer for Sports Illustrated (Brock); Justin Edwards/Getty Images (Hamilton); Focus on Sport/Getty Images (Wills); National Baseball Hall of Fame Library/MLB Photos/Getty Images (Carey); AP (Aparicio); Diamond Images/Getty Images (Case)

PIONEERS Sports Studio Photos/Getty Images (Robinson); National Baseball Hall of Fame Library (Murakami, Bellan)

CHARACTERS AP (Dean); George Silk/Time Life Pictures/Getty Images (Paige); Bettmann/Corbis (Berra); Kidwiler Collection/Diamond Images/Getty Images (Drabowsky); Rogers Photo Archive/Getty Images (Johnstone); J.D. Cuban/Getty Images (McDowell); Larry Goren/WireImage.com (Ramirez); Jason O. Watson/Getty Images (Scioscia)

MILESTONES National Baseball Hall of Fame Library/MLB Photos/Getty Images (Galvin); Al Tielemans for Sports Illustrated (Randy Johnson); Culver Pictures (Walter Johnson); Jim McIsaac/Getty Images (Smoltz); William C. Greene/TSN/Icon Sportswire (Ruth); John Biever for Sports Illustrated (Pujols); Mark Rucker/Transcendental Graphics/Getty Images (Anson); Patrick Smith/Getty Images (Rodriguez)

MANAGERS Bettmann/Corbis (Mack); AP (McCarthy); David Kohl/AP (Piniella); Aaron Harris/AP (Cox)

STRATEGIES Tom Watson/NY Daily News/Getty Images (Skowron); Bettmann/Corbis (Collins); Heinz Kluetmeier for Sports Illustrated (Palmer); Photo File/Getty Images (Powell); Focus on Sport/Getty Images (McGee); Pat Sullivan/AP (Ramirez)

UMPIRES National Baseball Hall of Fame Library (1880s); Chicago Daily News Inc./Chicago History Museum (1900s); Rogers Photo Archive/Getty Images (1960s); Rich Pilling/MLB Photos/Getty Images (1970s); Jonathan Daniel/Getty Images (1980s–90s); Tom Szczerbowski/Getty Images (today)

LEAGUES OF THEIR OWN National Baseball Hall of Fame Library/MLB Photos/Getty Images (Rickey, Bell); Bettmann/Corbis (DiMaggio); Historical Society for Southeast New Mexico (Bauman); Rich Schultz/AP (Jeter); National Baseball Hall of Fame Library (Daisies, Gibson, Crawfords); National Baseball Hall of Fame Library/AP (Kameshek); Transcendental Graphics/Getty Images (Foster)

DYNASTIES AP (1920s); Kidwiler Collection/Diamond Images/Getty Images (1930s); AP (1950s); Mark Lennihan/AP (1990s); Mark Rucker/Transcendental Graphics/Getty Images (Browns, Cardinals); Rogers Photo Archive/Getty Images (Athletics); National Baseball Hall of Fame Library/MLB Photos/Getty Images (NY Giants); Mark Kauffman for Sports Illustrated (Dodgers); Tony Triolo for Sports Illustrated (A's); Jamie Squire/Getty Images (SF Giants)

THE NAME GAME National Baseball Hall of Fame Library (Ruth candy bar, Williams fishing equipment, Sosa's cereal); Chuck Solomon for Sports Illustrated (Jackson candy bar); Courtesy of Nike (Jackson's kicks); Courtesy of PLBSports.com (Votto's cereal)

BASEBALL CARDS Mark Rucker/Transcendental Graphics/Getty Images (Hamilton); Transcendental Graphics/Getty Images (Ward, Young, Jackson, Ruth); AP (Wagner); Corbis (Speaker, Mathewson); Donruss (Ruth time line); Courtesy of Topps Company, Inc. (Clemente, 2000s, 2009, today); Fleer (Puckett); Pinnacle Brands (Jeter); Upper Deck (Larkin)

GAME TIME The Baseball Games Group (The Champion Game); Courtesy John Rose (All-Star Baseball, 2); Tomasz/Pietryszek/Getty Images (TV); Tengen (R.B.I. Baseball screen grab, box cover); Sablin/iStockPhoto/Getty Images (monitor)

YOU'RE UP Cincinnati Museum Center/Getty Images (stickball); Yale Joel/The Life Picture Collection/Getty Images (Little League); America 24-7/Getty Images (T-ball); Steve Wisbauer/Getty Images (Wiffle ball); Courtesy Joan Chandler (softball); Damian Strohmeyer for Sports Illustrated (Little League World Series)

GAME DAY PERKS AP (1940s); Corbis (1948); Walter Kelleher/NY Daily News/Getty Images (1952); NodderExchange.com (1960s); Andre/Fotolia.com (1990s); Michael Caulfield/AP (1995); Courtesy of the Chicago Cubs (1997 Beanie Baby, 2014 Etch A Sketch); Ben VanHouten/Seattle Mariners (1997); Chevrolet (2006); Erin Kirkland/Boston Red Sox (2014); Courtesy of Tampa Bay Rays (2015)

BALLPARK FOOD Alistair Cotton/iStockphoto/Getty Images (1930s); Diane Diedrich/Getty Images (1940s); Danny Moloshok/Icon Sportswire (Dodger Dogs); Lauri Patterson/Getty Images (hot dog); Barry Wong/Getty Images (pizza slice); John Biever for Sports Illustrated (sausage race); Pete Souza for Sports Illustrated (barbecue); Keith Torriel/NY Daily News Archive/Getty Images (2000s); Rob Tringali/Sportschrome/Getty Images (2010s)

BACK COVER Bret Wills for Sports Illustrated (5); Susan Einstein for Sports Illustrated (1); Milo Stewart/National Baseball Hall of Fame Library (2)